Python for Web Development: Build Websites with Django

A Step-by-Step Guide to Building Secure and Scalable Web Apps

BOOZMAN RICHARD

BOOKER BLUNT

Table of Content

TABLE OF CONTENTS

INTRODUCTION

Python for web development landscape has evolved dramatically over the past decade, with JavaScript frameworks playing a pivotal role in shaping how developers build interactive, dynamic, and scalable applications. In this rapidly changing ecosystem, staying up to date with the latest frameworks and technologies is crucial to building high-performance web applications that meet user expectations for speed, reliability, and seamless experiences across devices.

This book, *Python for web development Build with Django* is designed to be your comprehensive guide to mastering the most popular JavaScript frameworks used in modern web development. Whether you are just starting your journey into web development or you're a seasoned developer looking to deepen your knowledge, this book covers everything you need to know about **React**, **Angular**, and **Vue.js**. Each chapter is crafted to provide you with a clear understanding of the core concepts, best practices, and real-world examples, helping you build scalable, maintainable, and performant applications.

Why This Book Is Essential

The demand for rich, interactive web applications has never been higher. With the rise of Single Page Applications (SPAs), Progressive Web Apps (PWAs), and mobile-first design, developers must not only understand the principles of front-end development but also leverage modern JavaScript frameworks to enhance the user experience and meet the growing demands of today's digital world.

In this book, you will:

- Gain a deep understanding of **React**, **Angular**, and **Vue.js**, each of which has its unique strengths and weaknesses.
- Learn how to implement best practices for building fast, efficient, and secure web applications.
- Dive into advanced topics such as **state management**, **routing**, **service workers**, and **performance optimization**.
- Explore real-world examples of building web apps from scratch, including integrating APIs, securing user data, and optimizing performance.

- Get hands-on experience with building **Progressive Web Apps (PWAs)**, **Single Page Applications (SPAs)**, and mobile-first web solutions.

Whether you're looking to improve your skills in building scalable front-end applications or need to stay updated with the latest trends and technologies in web development, this book will serve as your essential companion.

What You Will Learn

In the first part of the book, we'll explore the foundational concepts of JavaScript frameworks. You'll get acquainted with the core principles behind **React**, **Angular**, and **Vue.js**, including their strengths, weaknesses, and appropriate use cases. We'll dive into the fundamentals of each framework, helping you choose the right tool for your next project.

Next, we will cover how to build real-world applications with these frameworks. You'll learn how to develop powerful web apps by creating dynamic user interfaces, managing state effectively, and implementing modern features like **routing**, **authentication**, and **data binding**. You'll also get hands-on experience building **single-page**

applications (SPAs) and integrating APIs to enhance the functionality of your app.

As we move deeper into advanced topics, the book will guide you through **state management** using libraries like **Redux** for React, **NgRx** for Angular, and **Vuex** for Vue.js. We'll also focus on performance optimization techniques such as **code splitting**, **lazy loading**, **caching**, and **progressive web apps (PWAs)** to ensure that your web apps perform at their best across all devices and network conditions.

Security is also a major concern when developing web applications. In this book, we'll explore how to protect your app from common vulnerabilities like **Cross-Site Scripting (XSS)**, **Cross-Site Request Forgery (CSRF)**, and **SQL Injection**. You'll learn how to implement secure authentication systems using **JWT** (JSON Web Tokens) and other modern techniques to safeguard your app's data and user privacy.

The final section of the book covers best practices and strategies for maintaining and evolving your web apps. We'll focus on **test-driven development (TDD)**, **unit testing**, and **end-to-end testing** with tools like **Jest**, **Karma**, and **Protractor**. We'll also discuss how to stay up to date with the latest trends and frameworks in the JavaScript ecosystem, ensuring your skills remain relevant in the ever-changing world of web development.

Who This Book Is For

This book is intended for developers of all experience levels who want to master modern JavaScript frameworks. Whether you are:

- A **beginner** looking to get started with React, Angular, or Vue.js, and want to learn the fundamentals of web development with modern frameworks.
- An **intermediate developer** who wants to deepen your understanding of state management, routing, testing, and performance optimization.
- An **experienced developer** seeking to stay updated on the latest tools, best practices, and trends in JavaScript frameworks, and how to build scalable, secure, and high-performance web applications.

Why React, Angular, and Vue.js?

The three frameworks covered in this book—**React**, **Angular**, and **Vue.js**—are the most widely used and popular choices for building web applications today. Each framework has unique features, and understanding their strengths and use cases will help you choose the right one for your project.

- **React**: Known for its simplicity and flexibility, React is a **JavaScript library** for building user interfaces. Its component-based architecture and virtual DOM make it highly efficient for rendering dynamic UIs, and it is widely adopted for creating modern, fast web applications.

- **Angular**: Angular is a **full-fledged framework** that provides everything you need for building large-scale web applications. With built-in tools like **dependency injection**, **routing**, and **forms management**, Angular is perfect for building complex, enterprise-level apps.

- **Vue.js**: Vue is a **progressive framework** that is both easy to learn and flexible enough to scale for large applications. It combines the best features of both React and Angular, offering an approachable learning curve with powerful tools for building dynamic, modern web apps.

By the end of this book, you'll have a solid understanding of these frameworks and the ability to build robust, production-ready web apps with them.

Conclusion

The world of JavaScript frameworks is constantly evolving, and staying up-to-date with the latest tools and techniques is essential for becoming a proficient web developer. *Mastering JavaScript Frameworks: From React to Angular* offers a detailed, hands-on guide to building modern web applications that are fast, scalable, and secure. By mastering these frameworks, you'll be equipped to tackle any web development challenge and stay at the forefront of the ever-changing landscape of web technologies.

Whether you're building a personal project or working on an enterprise-level application, the skills and knowledge you gain from this book will serve as a solid foundation for your future web development career. Let's dive in and explore the power of **React**, **Angular**, and **Vue.js**, and start building modern web apps that users love!

CHAPTER 1

INTRODUCTION TO WEB DEVELOPMENT WITH PYTHON AND DJANGO

Understanding Web Development Basics

Web development is the process of creating websites and web applications that run on the internet or an intranet. At its core, web development involves designing and developing the user interface, implementing server-side logic, and connecting to databases that store and manage data.

The world of web development can be broken down into two main components:

1. **Front-End Development**: This involves everything the user interacts with directly on the website. It includes the design, layout, and functionality visible in the browser, and uses technologies like HTML, CSS, and JavaScript to create interactive, user-friendly web pages.

2. **Back-End Development**: This is where the behind-the-scenes magic happens. Back-end developers work with server-side languages to build the logic, processes, and databases that drive the front end. They are responsible

for handling requests from users, processing the data, and sending the response back to the client.

The **full-stack** web developer is someone who works on both the front end and back end, bridging the gap between the two.

In this book, we will focus on **back-end development** using Python and Django, which is a powerful combination for creating robust and scalable web applications.

Overview of Python for Web Development

Python is a versatile and widely-used programming language that is known for its simplicity, readability, and vast ecosystem of libraries. Its concise syntax makes it an excellent choice for beginners while being powerful enough for experts to build sophisticated applications.

When it comes to web development, Python offers various frameworks, with **Django** being one of the most popular choices. Here's why Python is a great option for web development:

- **Easy to Learn and Read**: Python is known for its clear, straightforward syntax, which makes it an excellent choice for developers who are just starting.
- **Highly Scalable**: Python, especially with Django, is capable of handling large-scale applications, from small websites to complex enterprise solutions.

- **Rich Ecosystem and Libraries**: Python has a wealth of libraries and tools that make web development faster and more efficient. From data manipulation to machine learning, Python can be used for a wide variety of tasks beyond web development.
- **Strong Community**: Python has a large and active community of developers who contribute to its growth, providing a vast amount of tutorials, documentation, and third-party libraries.

Python's simplicity and power have made it the go-to language for many web developers who want to build efficient, reliable, and maintainable web applications.

Introduction to Django: What It Is and Why It's Popular

Django is a **high-level Python web framework** that encourages rapid development and clean, pragmatic design. It was created by developers who wanted to build web applications quickly without sacrificing the flexibility and power needed for complex projects.

Here's why Django has become a popular choice for developers:

- **Batteries Included**: Django is often described as a "batteries-included" framework because it comes with many built-in features, including an ORM (Object-Relational Mapper), an admin interface, and tools for security and authentication. This means you can focus on

16

writing the application code rather than reinventing the wheel.

- **Security**: Django is designed to help developers create secure websites. It has built-in protection against common security threats, such as cross-site scripting (XSS), cross-site request forgery (CSRF), SQL injection, and clickjacking.

- **Scalability**: Django has been used to build large-scale applications, including social networks and content management systems. Its scalability allows developers to scale applications as their needs grow.

- **Great Documentation**: Django's documentation is one of its standout features, offering detailed explanations of its features and best practices. This is especially useful for both beginners and experienced developers.

- **Active Community**: Django has a large and supportive community, with plenty of resources like forums, StackOverflow discussions, and meetups where developers can share knowledge.

Django makes web development more manageable by providing a solid framework that includes many tools, leaving you with more time to focus on your application's logic and functionality. Its design principles—such as reusability, rapid development, and scalability—make it an excellent choice for web developers of all levels.

Setting Up the Development Environment

To get started with Django, you'll need to set up your development environment. Here's a step-by-step guide on how to do this:

Step 1: Install Python

Before you can use Django, you need to have **Python** installed on your computer. You can download the latest version of Python from the official website: python.org. Make sure to check the box to add Python to your system's PATH during installation.

To verify that Python is installed, open a terminal or command prompt and type:

```bash
```

```bash
python --version
```

This should return the installed version of Python.

Step 2: Install Django

Once Python is installed, you can install Django using Python's package manager, **pip**. In your terminal or command prompt, type the following command:

```bash
```

```
pip install django
```

This command will download and install Django and its dependencies.

To verify the installation, you can check the installed version of Django by running:

```
bash
```

```
django-admin --version
```

Step 3: Create a Virtual Environment (Optional but Recommended)

It's good practice to use a **virtual environment** when working on Django projects. A virtual environment allows you to manage project-specific dependencies separately from the global Python environment.

To create a virtual environment:

1. Navigate to the directory where you want to store your project.
2. Run the following command to create a new virtual environment:

```
bash
```

```
python -m venv myenv
```

3. Activate the virtual environment:

- ○ **Windows**: `myenv\Scripts\activate`
- ○ **macOS/Linux**: `source myenv/bin/activate`

Once the virtual environment is activated, install Django within it:

bash

```
pip install django
```

Step 4: Create Your First Django Project

Now that you have Django installed, you can create a new Django project. To do this, use the following command in your terminal:

bash

```
django-admin startproject mysite
```

This will create a new directory called `mysite` containing the basic files for your project.

To run the project, navigate into the project directory:

bash

```
cd mysite
```

Then start the development server:

```bash
bash
```

```bash
python manage.py runserver
```

You can now open your web browser and navigate to http://127.0.0.1:8000/ to see your new Django site in action.

In this chapter, you learned about the basics of web development, the role Python and Django play in web development, and how to set up your development environment to start building web applications. In the next chapter, we will dive deeper into Django's architecture and how to structure a Django project effectively.

If you have any questions or issues setting up your environment, feel free to refer to Django's excellent documentation or ask for help from the vibrant Django community!

CHAPTER 2

UNDERSTANDING THE MVC PATTERN AND DJANGO'S MVT ARCHITECTURE

The Model-View-Controller (MVC) Pattern Explained

The **Model-View-Controller (MVC)** design pattern is one of the most widely used architectural patterns in software development, particularly in web applications. It separates the application into three interconnected components: the **Model**, the **View**, and the **Controller**. The goal of the MVC pattern is to promote the separation of concerns, making the code easier to manage, maintain, and scale.

1. **Model**:
   - o The Model represents the data and the business logic of the application. It is responsible for interacting with the database, handling the logic for retrieving and storing data, and performing computations or other data manipulations.
   - o The Model does not directly interact with the user interface (UI); it simply represents the underlying data structure.
2. **View**:

- o The View is the user interface (UI) of the application. It is responsible for presenting data to the user and receiving user input. The View communicates with the Model to display the data in a user-friendly format.
- o The View is usually focused on rendering the UI elements and does not contain the business logic or data manipulation itself.

3. **Controller**:

- o The Controller acts as an intermediary between the Model and the View. It listens for user input and updates the View and Model accordingly. For example, when a user submits a form, the Controller will process the data, update the Model, and refresh the View to reflect any changes.
- o The Controller contains the logic that drives the application's flow, such as user input handling, actions based on user requests, and the coordination of the View and Model.

Flow in MVC:

1. The user interacts with the **View** (e.g., filling out a form).
2. The **Controller** receives the user input and processes it.
3. The **Model** is updated with the new data or business logic.
4. The **View** is updated to reflect the changes in the Model.

Django's Model-View-Template (MVT) Pattern

Django follows a slightly different pattern known as the **Model-View-Template (MVT)** pattern. While it is similar to MVC, Django uses the term **Template** instead of **View** for the user interface component. The components of the MVT architecture are:

1. **Model**:
   - Just like in MVC, the Model in Django represents the data structure and handles the database operations. It defines the schema of the database tables and provides methods to query, update, or delete data. Django uses its **Object-Relational Mapper (ORM)** to map database tables to Python objects, allowing developers to interact with the database using Python code rather than writing raw SQL queries.
   - The Model is primarily concerned with the business logic and data manipulation.

2. **View**:
   - In Django's MVT pattern, the **View** is responsible for processing HTTP requests and returning HTTP responses. It contains the business logic for handling the user requests,

interacting with the Model, and returning the appropriate response.

- o Unlike MVC, where the View is strictly the UI layer, Django's View is more like the Controller in the traditional MVC pattern. The View receives data from the Model, applies the necessary logic, and passes it to the Template (UI) for rendering.

3. **Template**:
   - o The Template in Django is similar to the View in MVC. It is responsible for rendering HTML pages to be displayed to the user. Templates define the structure and layout of the UI, often using Django's templating language to embed dynamic data into HTML.
   - o Templates are used to display content, such as user information, blog posts, or any other data from the Model, in a clean and readable format for the user.

Flow in MVT:

1. The user makes a request to the **View** (e.g., visiting a URL or submitting a form).
2. The **View** processes the request, interacts with the **Model** to retrieve or modify data, and then renders the appropriate **Template**.

3. The **Template** generates the HTML page to be displayed to the user, which is returned as an HTTP response.

How the MVT Pattern Improves Web App Development

Django's MVT architecture improves web app development in several ways, making it an ideal framework for rapid, secure, and scalable web development:

1. **Separation of Concerns**:
   o By dividing the application into three distinct components (Model, View, and Template), Django enforces a clear separation of concerns. This makes the code more modular, allowing for easier maintenance and modification of each component independently. For example, if you need to update the user interface (Template), you can do so without affecting the business logic (Model) or the request handling (View).

2. **Reusability and Modularity**:
   o The MVT architecture promotes **reusability** of code. For instance, the same **Model** can be used across different Views or Templates. If you have a database table representing blog posts, you can use the same Model in different views, such as a

26

list of posts or a detailed post view, without having to duplicate the logic.

o   Similarly, Templates are reusable across different Views, making it easy to maintain a consistent user interface across the application.

3. **Efficiency and Speed**:

o   The **Template** layer in Django makes it easier to integrate dynamic content with static HTML. Django's templating language allows you to insert data directly into the HTML, reducing the time spent writing repetitive code.

o   Django's **ORM** allows for easy database management. You can interact with the database using Python code, without needing to write complex SQL queries. This leads to faster development and reduces the potential for errors.

4. **Security**:

o   Django's MVT pattern promotes security by handling common web development issues, such as cross-site scripting (XSS), SQL injection, and cross-site request forgery (CSRF). The framework automatically escapes data in Templates to prevent XSS attacks and provides tools for safely handling user inputs in Views.

o   Django's built-in user authentication and authorization system are part of the **View** layer, making it easier to manage secure access to different parts of your app.

5. **Scalability and Maintenance**:

o Django's MVT pattern is designed to handle large-scale applications. By separating the responsibilities of the Model, View, and Template, you can scale your application in a modular way. As the app grows, you can continue to modify and add features to each component without affecting the others.

o Django also supports **modular development** with reusable components, which is essential for building complex web applications that need to scale over time.

6. **Built-in Tools**:

o Django comes with a variety of built-in tools and features that enhance the development experience. These include the Django admin interface (which allows you to manage content easily), form handling, URL routing, and much more. These tools work seamlessly with the MVT architecture, allowing for quicker and more efficient development.

In summary, while Django follows a slightly different pattern—Model-View-Template (MVT)—than the traditional Model-View-Controller (MVC) pattern, the fundamental principles of separation of concerns and modularity remain the same. By understanding the MVT architecture, you gain insight into how Django organizes web applications and how it allows you to build robust, secure, and scalable web applications efficiently.

In the next chapter, we will dive deeper into Django's project structure, explaining the files and configurations that help make Django a powerful web framework.

CHAPTER 3

SETTING UP A DJANGO PROJECT

Installing Django and Setting Up a New Project

Before you can begin developing web applications with Django, you need to install Django and create your first project. Django is easy to install and set up, and it comes with everything you need to start building web applications.

Step 1: Install Python

As a prerequisite, make sure Python is installed on your system. Django is a Python web framework, so Python must be installed first. You can download the latest version of Python from the official website: python.org.

To check if Python is already installed, open a terminal or command prompt and run the following command:

```bash

python --version
```

If Python is not installed, download and install it from the website above.

Step 2: Install Django

Once Python is installed, the next step is to install Django using the package manager **pip**. Pip is bundled with Python, so you can easily install Django by running the following command:

```bash
```

```bash
pip install django
```

This command will download and install the latest version of Django and all the dependencies required for your web development environment.

To verify that Django was installed correctly, run:

```bash
```

```bash
django-admin --version
```

This should return the installed version of Django.

Step 3: Create a New Django Project

Once Django is installed, you can create a new project by running the following command:

```bash
```

```bash
django-admin startproject mysite
```

Replace `mysite` with the name of your project. This command creates a new directory called `mysite` containing the basic structure of a Django project.

Navigate into your new project directory:

```bash

cd mysite
```
Step 4: Start the Development Server

Now that the project is set up, you can run Django's built-in development server to see your project in action. Run the following command:

```bash

python manage.py runserver
```

This will start a local development server. By default, Django will run on port 8000. Open a web browser and navigate to http://127.0.0.1:8000/ to see the Django welcome page. If you see the "Congratulations" page, then your Django project is successfully set up!

Introduction to Django's File Structure

Once you've created a Django project, you'll notice a directory structure that may seem a bit different from other types of Python projects. Django organizes the project in a way that helps separate concerns and makes it easier to manage large projects. Here's an overview of the files and directories created when you start a Django project:

```
markdown

mysite/
|
├── manage.py
├── mysite/
|    ├── __init__.py
|    ├── settings.py
|    ├── urls.py
|    ├── asgi.py
|    └── wsgi.py
```

- **manage.py**: This is a command-line utility that helps you manage various Django tasks. It allows you to interact with the project through the terminal, such as running the development server, applying database migrations, and creating new apps. You will use `manage.py` for almost all of your interactions with the Django project.

- **mysite/**: This directory contains the main Django project folder. It includes the core configuration files for your project.
  - **init.py**: This file tells Python that this directory should be treated as a Python package.
  - **settings.py**: This file contains the main settings for your Django project, such as database configuration, installed apps, middleware, templates, static files, etc.
  - **urls.py**: This file is where you define the URL patterns for your project. It maps URLs to views, helping to determine what the user sees when they visit specific pages of your web application.
  - **asgi.py**: This is the entry point for ASGI-compatible web servers. ASGI stands for Asynchronous Server Gateway Interface and is used for handling asynchronous requests in modern web applications.
  - **wsgi.py**: Similar to `asgi.py`, this is the entry point for WSGI-compatible web servers. WSGI stands for Web Server Gateway Interface and is the standard for synchronous web applications.

These files work together to form the foundation of your Django project.

Basic Configuration of Your First Django Project

After creating a new Django project and understanding the basic file structure, the next step is configuring the project to get it ready for development. Let's go over some key configuration tasks that are typically performed early on in the project setup.

Step 1: Configure the Database

Django uses an Object-Relational Mapper (ORM) to interact with databases. By default, Django is configured to use **SQLite**, which is a lightweight, file-based database that doesn't require complex setup.

In the `settings.py` file, you will find the following default database configuration:

```python
DATABASES = {
    'default': {
        'ENGINE': 'django.db.backends.sqlite3',
        'NAME': BASE_DIR / 'db.sqlite3',
    }
}
```

This means that your project is using SQLite by default. If you want to use a different database (such as PostgreSQL or MySQL), you would modify the DATABASES setting accordingly.

Step 2: Configure Static and Media Files

Static files are files like CSS, JavaScript, and images that are used in your website's frontend. Media files are files that users upload, such as profile pictures or documents.

In the `settings.py` file, you can configure Django's static and media file handling:

```python
python

# Static files (CSS, JavaScript, images)
STATIC_URL = '/static/'

# Media files (uploads)
MEDIA_URL = '/media/'
MEDIA_ROOT = BASE_DIR / 'media'
```

Django will automatically serve static files in development, but in production, you will need a web server (such as Nginx or Apache) to serve these files.

Step 3: Configure Allowed Hosts

The **ALLOWED_HOSTS** setting in `settings.py` defines which domains or IP addresses your Django project is allowed to serve. By default, it's set to an empty list, meaning your project will only be accessible on the local machine.

In a production environment, you will need to add your domain name or IP address to this list:

```python
```

```
ALLOWED_HOSTS        =        ['yourdomain.com',
'www.yourdomain.com']
```

Step 4: Configure the Secret Key

Django uses a **secret key** to provide cryptographic signing, and it is a critical part of keeping your application secure. This key is automatically generated when you create a new project, but in a production environment, you should make sure the key is kept secret and not hardcoded in your source code.

To manage the secret key securely, you can store it as an environment variable or use a third-party service like **Django-environ** to load it from a .env file.

```python
```

```
import os
SECRET_KEY = os.getenv('DJANGO_SECRET_KEY')
```

Step 5: Run Database Migrations

Django comes with a powerful migration system that helps you keep your database schema in sync with your models. After setting up your project, you'll need to apply the initial database migrations, which create the necessary tables for Django's built-in apps.

To do this, run the following command:

```
bash
```

```
python manage.py migrate
```

This will apply the default migrations and create the necessary database tables for things like authentication, sessions, and admin functionality.

Summary

In this chapter, we covered how to install Django and set up a new project, explored the structure of a Django project, and went through some basic configuration steps to get your project ready for development. These are the foundational steps to setting up a Django project, and from here, you can start adding your own apps, configuring your models, and building out the features of your web application.

In the next chapter, we'll dive deeper into Django's architecture, including how to define models, work with the database, and create your first Django app!

CHAPTER 4

DJANGO MODELS: WORKING WITH DATABASES

Introduction to Django Models and ORM (Object-Relational Mapping)

In Django, **models** are Python classes that define the structure of your database tables. Each model represents a table in the database, and each attribute of the model represents a field in that table. Django's **Object-Relational Mapping (ORM)** system allows you to interact with the database using Python code, without needing to write raw SQL queries. This makes database operations more intuitive and allows you to work with data in a more Pythonic way.

The **ORM** maps the data in your database to Python objects, making it easy to perform CRUD (Create, Read, Update, Delete) operations. For example, instead of writing SQL queries like `SELECT * FROM blog_posts`, you can use Django's ORM to retrieve all blog posts using simple Python code.

Defining Models, Fields, and Relationships

Defining a Model

In Django, models are defined by creating a Python class that inherits from `django.db.models.Model`. For example, let's define a simple model for a blog post:

```python
from django.db import models

class BlogPost(models.Model):
    title = models.CharField(max_length=200)   # A text field for the blog post title
    content = models.TextField()  # A text field for the blog post content
    author = models.CharField(max_length=100)   # A field for the author's name
    created_at = models.DateTimeField(auto_now_add=True)        # Automatically set the timestamp when the post is created
    updated_at = models.DateTimeField(auto_now=True)          # Automatically set the timestamp when the post is updated

    def __str__(self):
        return self.title
```

In this example:

- **CharField** is used for small text fields (e.g., `title`, `author`).
- **TextField** is used for larger text fields (e.g., `content`).
- **DateTimeField** is used to store date and time information.
- The `auto_now_add=True` parameter means that the `created_at` field will automatically be set when the blog post is created, and `auto_now=True` means the `updated_at` field will automatically update whenever the model is modified.

Fields in Models

Django provides several types of fields to represent different types of data. Some of the most common field types include:

- **CharField**: A short text field (e.g., title, name).
- **TextField**: A large text field (e.g., content, description).
- **IntegerField**: A field for storing integers.
- **DateTimeField**: A field for storing date and time information.
- **DecimalField**: A field for storing fixed-point decimal numbers.
- **ForeignKey**: A field used for creating a one-to-many relationship between models.

41

Defining Relationships Between Models

One of Django's greatest strengths is its ability to define relationships between models with its ORM. These relationships allow you to structure your database efficiently.

1. **One-to-Many Relationships** (using `ForeignKey`): A one-to-many relationship is where one record in one model is related to multiple records in another model. For example, one author can write many blog posts. To define this, you would use a `ForeignKey` in the related model (e.g., `BlogPost`).

   python

   ```python
   class BlogPost(models.Model):
       title                          =
   models.CharField(max_length=200)
       content = models.TextField()
       author  =  models.ForeignKey('Author',
   on_delete=models.CASCADE)    # One-to-many
   relationship
   ```

   Here, the `ForeignKey` field establishes a relationship between `BlogPost` and `Author`, meaning each `BlogPost` is associated with one `Author`.

2. **Many-to-Many Relationships** (using `ManyToManyField`): A many-to-many relationship is where multiple records in one model are related to multiple records in another model. For example, a blog post can have many tags, and a tag can be associated with many blog posts. To define this, you would use a `ManyToManyField`.

```python
python

class Tag(models.Model):
    name = models.CharField(max_length=50)

class BlogPost(models.Model):
    title                         =
models.CharField(max_length=200)
    content = models.TextField()
    tags = models.ManyToManyField(Tag)   #
Many-to-many relationship
```

In this example, each `BlogPost` can have many `Tag` instances, and each `Tag` can be associated with many `BlogPost` instances.

3. **One-to-One Relationships** (using `OneToOneField`): A one-to-one relationship means one record in one model is related to one record in another model. For example, each

blog post may have one associated image. You can define this with a `OneToOneField`.

```python
python
```

```python
class BlogPost(models.Model):
    title                    =
models.CharField(max_length=200)
    content = models.TextField()


class BlogPostImage(models.Model):
    image                    =
models.ImageField(upload_to='blog_images/
')
    blog_post                =
models.OneToOneField(BlogPost,
on_delete=models.CASCADE)
```

In this case, each `BlogPostImage` is related to exactly one `BlogPost`.

Database Migrations and Schema Management

In Django, the **migrations** system is used to apply changes to your database schema. When you create or modify models, Django doesn't automatically update the database. Instead, it uses migrations to manage these changes.

Creating Migrations

Whenever you create or modify models, you need to generate a migration file that tells Django how to update the database schema. Run the following command:

```bash
```

```bash
python manage.py makemigrations
```

This will generate a migration file that contains the necessary changes to the database schema. Django will create a migration file in the `migrations/` directory of your app.

Applying Migrations

Once the migration files are created, you can apply them to update your database schema. To apply the migrations, run:

```bash
```

```bash
python manage.py migrate
```

This will update your database by applying all the pending migrations. You can also specify a specific app to apply migrations for by running:

```bash
```

```
python manage.py migrate <app_name>
```

Inspecting Migrations

If you want to see what migrations Django has applied, you can run:

```
bash
```

```
python manage.py showmigrations
```

This will list all migrations for your project and indicate whether each one has been applied.

Real-World Example: Building a Blog App Database

Let's apply what we've learned by building a simple database for a blog app. We'll define models for blog posts, authors, and tags. Here's how you can structure the database for a basic blog:

1. **Author Model**: This will represent the author of the blog post.
2. **BlogPost Model**: This will represent the blog posts, containing a title, content, and a reference to the author.
3. **Tag Model**: This will represent tags that can be associated with blog posts.

```
python
```

```python
# models.py

from django.db import models

# Author Model
class Author(models.Model):
    name = models.CharField(max_length=100)
    bio = models.TextField()

    def __str__(self):
        return self.name

# BlogPost Model
class BlogPost(models.Model):
    title = models.CharField(max_length=200)
    content = models.TextField()
    author        =        models.ForeignKey(Author,
on_delete=models.CASCADE)
    created_at                              =
models.DateTimeField(auto_now_add=True)
    updated_at                              =
models.DateTimeField(auto_now=True)
    tags = models.ManyToManyField('Tag')

    def __str__(self):
        return self.title

# Tag Model
```

```
class Tag(models.Model):
    name = models.CharField(max_length=50)

    def __str__(self):
        return self.name
```

In this example:

- The `Author` model has fields for the author's name and bio.
- The `BlogPost` model has fields for the title, content, and timestamps, and it links to the `Author` model through a **ForeignKey**.
- The `Tag` model is used to store tags, which are related to blog posts via a **ManyToManyField**.

Once you've defined these models, you can run `makemigrations` and `migrate` to apply them to the database.

bash

```
python manage.py makemigrations
python manage.py migrate
```

This will create the database schema for the blog app. You can now start adding blog posts, authors, and tags to your application.

Summary

In this chapter, we explored Django's ORM and how to define models, fields, and relationships. We discussed the three main types of relationships in Django: **one-to-many**, **many-to-many**, and **one-to-one**. We also covered the process of creating and applying migrations to manage changes to the database schema.

The real-world example of building a blog app database helped us apply these concepts, creating models for blog posts, authors, and tags. With this knowledge, you are ready to work with databases in Django and start developing more complex applications.

In the next chapter, we will dive deeper into Django views, where we'll learn how to handle HTTP requests and display dynamic content to the user.

CHAPTER 5

DJANGO VIEWS: HANDLING USER REQUESTS

Overview of Django Views and How They Handle HTTP Requests

In Django, **views** are responsible for handling user requests and returning HTTP responses. When a user visits a URL in a Django web application, the request is processed by a view, which is essentially a Python function or class that determines what data should be displayed and how it should be presented. Views are the part of the application that processes user inputs, interacts with the models, and generates the HTML that the user sees.

Every time a user sends a request to the server (e.g., when they visit a URL), Django uses the **URLconf** (URL configuration) to match the request to the corresponding view. The view then processes the request and returns an HTTP response, which could be an HTML page, a redirect, a JSON response, or any other type of content.

Here is a basic example of how a Django view works:

- A user visits a URL, for example: `http://127.0.0.1:8000/blog/`.

- Django uses its URL patterns to find the corresponding view function.
- The view processes the request (such as fetching data from the database or handling form input).
- The view generates a response (such as rendering a template with data) and returns it to the user's browser.

Django views can be divided into two main types: **function-based views (FBV)** and **class-based views (CBV)**.

Function-Based Views (FBV) vs. Class-Based Views (CBV)

Function-Based Views (FBV)

A **function-based view** is the simplest and most straightforward type of view in Django. It is just a regular Python function that takes an HTTP request as a parameter and returns an HTTP response. The function is responsible for processing the request and returning the appropriate response.

Here's an example of a simple FBV that handles a request and returns a response:

```python

from django.http import HttpResponse

def blog_home(request):
```

```
return HttpResponse("Welcome to the Blog!")
```

In this example:

- The `blog_home` function is a view that receives an HTTP request and returns a simple text response: `"Welcome to the Blog!"`.
- `HttpResponse` is a class provided by Django to generate HTTP responses.

FBVs are great for simple views where the logic is straightforward and easy to handle. They are intuitive, and you can easily see what is happening in a single function.

Class-Based Views (CBV)

A **class-based view** is a more structured and reusable approach to defining views. CBVs are especially useful when you need to handle more complex interactions or when you want to follow object-oriented principles in your views. A class-based view is defined as a Python class that inherits from Django's built-in view classes, such as `View` or other specialized classes like `ListView`, `DetailView`, `CreateView`, etc.

Here's an example of a simple class-based view:

```python
```

```python
from django.http import HttpResponse
from django.views import View

class BlogHomeView(View):
    def get(self, request):
        return HttpResponse("Welcome to the
Blog!")
```

In this example:

- `BlogHomeView` is a class that inherits from Django's `View` class.

- The `get` method is called when the user sends a GET request to the view, and it returns an HTTP response.

- CBVs can have different methods (like `get`, `post`, etc.) to handle different types of HTTP requests (GET, POST, etc.).

While FBVs are simple and straightforward, CBVs offer greater flexibility, organization, and reusability. They are often preferred for more complex applications where views need to handle a variety of different tasks, such as displaying lists, handling forms, or performing CRUD operations.

Real-World Example: Creating Views for a Blog App

Let's walk through a real-world example of creating views for a blog app. We'll create views for displaying a list of blog posts and viewing the details of a single blog post. We'll demonstrate both **function-based views (FBV)** and **class-based views (CBV)**.

Step 1: Creating the BlogPost Model

Before we create the views, let's define a `BlogPost` model in `models.py` to represent the blog posts:

python

```python
from django.db import models

class BlogPost(models.Model):
    title = models.CharField(max_length=200)
    content = models.TextField()
    created_at                              =
models.DateTimeField(auto_now_add=True)

    def __str__(self):
        return self.title
```

This model has three fields: `title`, `content`, and `created_at`, and it is used to store blog post data in the database.

Step 2: Creating Views to Display Blog Posts

Option 1: Using Function-Based Views (FBV)

First, let's create a function-based view to display a list of all blog posts:

```python
python
```

```python
from django.shortcuts import render
from .models import BlogPost

def blog_list(request):
    posts = BlogPost.objects.all()  # Fetch all blog posts from the database
    return                          render(request,
'blog/blog_list.html', {'posts': posts})
```

In this view:

- We use `BlogPost.objects.all()` to fetch all the blog posts from the database.
- We then render a template called `blog_list.html` and pass the `posts` queryset to the template using the context (`{'posts': posts}`).

Next, let's create a view to display the details of a single blog post:

```python
python
```

```python
from     django.shortcuts      import     render,
get_object_or_404
from .models import BlogPost


def blog_detail(request, pk):
    post = get_object_or_404(BlogPost, pk=pk)    #
Get the blog post by primary key (pk)
    return                        render(request,
'blog/blog_detail.html', {'post': post})
```

In this view:

- We use `get_object_or_404` to fetch a single blog post based on its primary key (`pk`).
- We render the `blog_detail.html` template and pass the `post` object to the template.

Option 2: Using Class-Based Views (CBV)

Now, let's achieve the same functionality using class-based views.

1. **Blog List View**: Display a list of all blog posts.

```python
python
```

```python
from django.views.generic import ListView
from .models import BlogPost


class BlogListView(ListView):
```

56

```
model = BlogPost
template_name = 'blog/blog_list.html'
context_object_name = 'posts'
```

In this CBV:

- We inherit from `ListView`, a generic view that automatically handles fetching a list of objects (in this case, `BlogPost`).
- `template_name` specifies the template to render, and `context_object_name` sets the name of the variable that will be passed to the template.

2. **Blog Detail View**: Display the details of a single blog post.

python

```
from django.views.generic import DetailView
from .models import BlogPost

class BlogDetailView(DetailView):
    model = BlogPost
    template_name = 'blog/blog_detail.html'
    context_object_name = 'post'
```

In this CBV:

- We inherit from `DetailView`, a generic view that automatically fetches a single object based on the primary key.
- `template_name` specifies the template to render, and `context_object_name` sets the name of the variable that will be passed to the template.

Step 3: Configuring URLs

Now, let's create the URL patterns that map to these views. In `urls.py`, we define the URLs for the blog list and blog detail views:

python

```python
from django.urls import path
from . import views

urlpatterns = [
    path('', views.blog_list, name='blog_list'),
# For function-based view
    path('<int:pk>/',          views.blog_detail,
name='blog_detail'),   # For function-based view
]
```

For the class-based views, the URL configuration would look like this:

python

```
from django.urls import path
from .views import BlogListView, BlogDetailView

urlpatterns = [
    path('',                    BlogListView.as_view(),
name='blog_list'),  # For class-based view
    path('<int:pk>/', BlogDetailView.as_view(),
name='blog_detail'),  # For class-based view
]
```

Summary

In this chapter, we explored how Django views handle HTTP requests and generate responses. We discussed the two main types of views in Django: **function-based views (FBV)** and **class-based views (CBV)**, highlighting the differences between them. While FBVs are simple and easy to understand, CBVs offer more structure and reusability for complex applications.

We also created real-world views for a blog app, including a list of blog posts and a detail page for each post. We implemented both FBVs and CBVs to demonstrate how each approach can be used to handle user requests.

In the next chapter, we will dive into Django templates and how they can be used to display dynamic content to users in a clean and maintainable way.

CHAPTER 6

DJANGO TEMPLATES: RENDERING HTML PAGES

Understanding Django Templates and Templating Language

In Django, **templates** are used to define the structure and layout of HTML pages. Django's **templating language** allows you to insert dynamic content into your HTML, making it possible to render data from models, display content based on user interaction, and even loop over lists of objects.

Django templates are separate from views and models, and their primary purpose is to present the data to the user. The idea is to keep the presentation layer (HTML) separated from the logic layer (views and models). By using Django templates, you can create dynamic web pages that change based on the data they receive.

Template Syntax

Django's templating language is simple and intuitive. It uses the following basic syntax:

- **Variables**: Variables are enclosed in double curly braces {{ }}. These are placeholders for dynamic content that you want to display in the HTML page. For example:

```
html
```

```
<h1>{{ post.title }}</h1>
<p>{{ post.content }}</p>
```

This will render the `title` and `content` of a blog post.

- **Template Tags**: Template tags are enclosed in `{% %}` and provide control over the logic in your templates. For example:

```
html
```

```
{% if post.author %}
  <p>Written by: {{ post.author }}</p>
{% else %}
  <p>Anonymous Author</p>
{% endif %}
```

This will check if the post has an `author` and display the author's name. If no author exists, it will display "Anonymous Author."

- **Template Filters**: Filters are applied to variables to modify the displayed output. They are added using a pipe `|` symbol. For example:

```
html
```

```
<p>{{ post.created_at|date:"F j, Y" }}</p>
```

This will display the `created_at` date of the post in the format "Month day, Year."

Templates are typically stored in the `templates/` directory of your Django app, and Django automatically looks for templates within this directory when rendering a view.

Using Template Tags, Filters, and Static Files

Template Tags

Template tags are essential for adding control logic to templates. Some common template tags include:

- **{% if %}** and **{% endif %}**: These tags are used for conditional statements. You can use them to display content only if a certain condition is met.

Example:

html

```
{% if user.is_authenticated %}
  <p>Welcome, {{ user.username }}!</p>
{% else %}
  <p>Please log in.</p>
{% endif %}
```

63

- **{% for %}** and **{% endfor %}**: These tags are used for looping through a list of objects. For example, you can loop through a list of blog posts and display each one on the page.

Example:

html

```
{% for post in posts %}
  <h2>{{ post.title }}</h2>
  <p>{{ post.content }}</p>
{% empty %}
  <p>No posts available.</p>
{% endfor %}
```

- **{% include %}**: This tag is used to include one template within another. It's useful for breaking down large templates into smaller, reusable components.

Example:

html

```
{% include "header.html" %}
```

- **{% block %}** and **{% endblock %}**: These tags are used in a base template to define sections of the template that can be overridden in child templates. This is useful for maintaining a consistent layout across multiple pages.

Example (in a base template):

html

```
<html>
  <head>
    <title>{% block title %}My Blog{%
endblock %}</title>
  </head>
  <body>
    <header>{% include "navbar.html"
%}</header>
    <div>{% block content %}{% endblock
%}</div>
  </body>
</html>
```

Example (in a child template):

html

```
{% extends "base.html" %}
{% block content %}
  <h1>Welcome to the Blog</h1>
  <p>This is the homepage.</p>
{% endblock %}
```

Template Filters

Template filters modify the display of a variable's value. Some useful filters include:

- **date**: Formats date and time values.

  html

  ```
  <p>{{ post.created_at|date:"F j, Y" }}</p>
  ```

- **length**: Returns the length of an object.

  html

  ```
  <p>The number of blog posts is: {{ posts|length }}</p>
  ```

- **lower and upper**: Converts a string to lowercase or uppercase.

  html

  ```
  <p>{{ post.title|lower }}</p>
  ```

- **default**: Provides a default value if the variable is empty or None.

  html

```
<p>{{       post.author|default:"Anonymous"
}}</p>
```

Static Files

Static files are the resources (like CSS, JavaScript, and images) used by the front-end of the website. These files are different from dynamic content generated by views and templates. In Django, static files are handled separately from templates.

To serve static files in development:

1. Create a directory called `static/` within your app.
2. Add your static files (e.g., CSS or JavaScript files) to this directory.

To link a static file in a template, use the `{% static %}` tag:

```
html
```

```
{% load static %}
<link    rel="stylesheet"    href="{%    static
'css/styles.css' %}">
```

This will render the path to your static CSS file.

To include images in your template:

```
html
```

67

```
<img  src="{%  static  'images/logo.png'  %}"
alt="Logo">
```

In production, you would need to set up a web server (like Nginx or Apache) to serve static files more efficiently. But during development, Django automatically handles static files for you.

Real-World Example: Creating a Dynamic Homepage for a Blog

Let's create a dynamic homepage for a blog using Django templates. Our homepage will display the latest blog posts and show some dynamic content based on the data in the database.

Step 1: Define the View

In your views.py file, define the view for the homepage:

python

```
from django.shortcuts import render
from .models import BlogPost

def home(request):
    # Fetch the latest 5 blog posts
    posts = BlogPost.objects.all().order_by('-
created_at')[:5]
    return render(request, 'blog/home.html',
{'posts': posts})
```

In this view:

- We fetch the latest 5 blog posts from the `BlogPost` model, ordered by the creation date in descending order.
- We pass the `posts` queryset to the template.

Step 2: Create the Template

Next, create the `home.html` template in the `templates/blog/` directory:

html

```
{% extends "base.html" %}

{% block title %}Welcome to the Blog{% endblock %}

{% block content %}
  <h1>Latest Blog Posts</h1>
  {% for post in posts %}
    <div class="post">
      <h2>{{ post.title }}</h2>
      <p>{{ post.content|slice:":100" }}...</p>
<!-- Displaying the first 100 characters of
content -->
      <p><a href="{% url 'blog_detail' post.pk
%}">Read more</a></p>
    </div>
```

```
{% empty %}
    <p>No blog posts available.</p>
  {% endfor %}
{% endblock %}
```

In this template:

- We extend the `base.html` template, which contains the common structure for all pages.
- Inside the `{% block content %}`, we loop over the `posts` variable and display each blog post's title and the first 100 characters of the content.
- We provide a link to the blog post detail page using `{% url 'blog_detail' post.pk %}`.

Step 3: Add URL Pattern

Finally, define a URL pattern for the homepage in `urls.py`:

python

```python
from django.urls import path
from . import views

urlpatterns = [
    path('', views.home, name='home'),      # Homepage URL
    path('<int:pk>/', views.blog_detail, name='blog_detail'),  # Detail page URL
```

]

Now, when a user visits the homepage (e.g., `http://127.0.0.1:8000/`), they will see the latest blog posts, and if they click the "Read more" link, they will be taken to the detail page for each post.

Summary

In this chapter, we explored Django templates and the templating language that allows you to dynamically render HTML pages. We learned about **template tags**, which provide logic in templates, **filters**, which modify the output of variables, and how to include **static files** like CSS and images.

We also worked through a real-world example of creating a dynamic homepage for a blog. This included rendering the latest blog posts using a function-based view and Django templates, displaying dynamic content, and linking to a detail page.

In the next chapter, we'll focus on working with forms in Django, learning how to handle user input, validate it, and process form submissions effectively.

CHAPTER 7

URL ROUTING AND HANDLING REQUESTS

Introduction to URL Routing in Django

In Django, **URL routing** is the mechanism that maps an incoming web request (such as a user visiting a specific URL) to a corresponding view. URL routing is a core part of how Django handles user interactions. When a user visits a URL, Django uses its URL routing system to determine which view should process the request and return a response.

In Django, URL routing is defined in a file called `urls.py`, which is where you define the URL patterns and their associated views. Django's URL dispatcher matches a user's request to a URL pattern and forwards it to the appropriate view function or class-based view.

By default, Django looks for a `urls.py` file in each application and in the main project folder. This allows you to create modular URL routing that can be reused and extended across different apps.

The URL routing system is flexible, allowing you to define simple static URLs or more complex dynamic URLs that include variables (e.g., a blog post's unique identifier).

Creating URL Patterns and Mapping Views

In Django, URL patterns are defined using regular expressions, which are used to match parts of the URL. Each URL pattern corresponds to a view, which is a Python function or class that handles the request and generates an HTTP response.

Step 1: Define URL Patterns

A URL pattern is defined as a path that a user can visit. URL patterns are defined in a list inside the `urls.py` file. Here's a simple example:

python

```
# urls.py

from django.urls import path
from . import views

urlpatterns = [
    path('home/', views.home, name='home'),   #
Map 'home/' to the 'home' view
]
```

In this example:

- `path('home/', views.home, name='home')` maps the URL `home/` to the `home` view.
- The `name='home'` argument allows you to refer to this URL by name in templates and other parts of the application (more on this in a moment).

Step 2: Dynamic URL Patterns

Django allows you to define **dynamic** URLs that can capture parts of the URL and pass them as arguments to the view. This is done using **converter types**.

For example, if we want to create a URL pattern for a blog post detail page where the URL includes the blog post's ID, we can use the following pattern:

python

```
# urls.py

from django.urls import path
from . import views

urlpatterns = [
    path('post/<int:pk>/',    views.blog_detail,
name='blog_detail'),   # Dynamic URL for a blog
post
```

74

]

In this example:

- `<int:pk>` is a dynamic part of the URL, where `<int:pk>` is a **path converter**. The `<int>` part means the URL expects an integer value, and `pk` is the name of the variable that will be passed to the view.
- `views.blog_detail` is the view function that will process the request and render the blog post based on the `pk` (primary key) provided in the URL.

Step 3: Using Regular Expressions for Advanced Routing

While the `path()` function is great for simple routing, you can also use **regular expressions** to create more complex URL patterns. Django provides a `re_path()` function that allows you to use regular expressions in URL patterns.

Example of a regular expression-based URL pattern:

```python
# urls.py

from django.urls import re_path
from . import views

urlpatterns = [
```

```
    re_path(r'^post/(?P<pk>\d+)/$',
views.blog_detail, name='blog_detail'),
]
```

In this example:

- `re_path()` uses a regular expression to capture the `pk` from the URL.
- The regular expression `(?P<pk>\d+)` matches one or more digits (`\d+`) and passes them to the view as the `pk` argument.

Note: Regular expressions are more powerful but can be more complex and harder to read, so they are generally used for more advanced URL routing.

Real-World Example: URL Patterns for a Blog App

Let's now look at a real-world example of how you might set up URL patterns for a simple blog application. In this example, we'll define URLs for the homepage, individual blog posts, and creating new blog posts.

Step 1: Define the Views

We'll first define the views in `views.py` for listing blog posts and viewing a single blog post.

```python
python
```

```python
# views.py

from django.shortcuts import render,
get_object_or_404
from .models import BlogPost

def home(request):
    # Fetch all blog posts
    posts = BlogPost.objects.all().order_by('-
created_at')
    return render(request, 'blog/home.html',
{'posts': posts})

def blog_detail(request, pk):
    # Fetch a single blog post by primary key
    post = get_object_or_404(BlogPost, pk=pk)
    return                    render(request,
'blog/blog_detail.html', {'post': post})

def create_blog_post(request):
    # Placeholder function for creating a new
blog post
    return                    render(request,
'blog/create_blog_post.html')
```

In this example:

- home fetches all blog posts and displays them in a list.

- `blog_detail` fetches a single blog post based on the `pk` and displays the details.

- `create_blog_post` is a placeholder function for creating new blog posts (we'll discuss form handling in a later chapter).

Step 2: Define URL Patterns

Next, we'll define the URL patterns in `urls.py` to map URLs to these views:

```python
# urls.py

from django.urls import path
from . import views

urlpatterns = [
    path('', views.home, name='home'),       # Homepage with list of blog posts
    path('post/<int:pk>/', views.blog_detail, name='blog_detail'),  # Blog post detail page
    path('post/create/', views.create_blog_post, name='create_blog_post'),  # Page to create new blog post
]
```

Here's what each pattern does:

- `path('', views.home, name='home')`: This maps the root URL (/) to the `home` view, which displays a list of all blog posts.
- `path('post/<int:pk>/', views.blog_detail, name='blog_detail')`: This maps the URL `post/<pk>/` to the `blog_detail` view, where `<int:pk>` is the primary key of the blog post.
- `path('post/create/', views.create_blog_post, name='create_blog_post')`: This maps the URL `post/create/` to the `create_blog_post` view, which will be used to create new blog posts.

Step 3: Configuring Templates

Now let's create the corresponding templates to display the blog posts. We'll start with the homepage template (`home.html`).

html

```
<!-- home.html -->

{% extends "base.html" %}

{% block title %}Home{% endblock %}

{% block content %}
  <h1>Latest Blog Posts</h1>
```

```
{% for post in posts %}
  <div class="post">
    <h2><a href="{% url 'blog_detail' post.pk
%}">{{ post.title }}</a></h2>
      <p>{{ post.content|slice:":100" }}...</p>
<!-- Display first 100 characters -->
  </div>
{% empty %}
  <p>No blog posts available.</p>
{% endfor %}
{% endblock %}
```

In this template:

- We extend a base template (base.html), which includes common layout elements (like the header and footer).
- We loop through the posts passed from the view and display the title and the first 100 characters of the content.
- The href="{% url 'blog_detail' post.pk %}" generates a dynamic URL for the blog_detail view based on the pk of each post.

Step 4: Create URL Links in Templates

To link to the blog post creation page, you can add the following code to any template, such as home.html:

html

```
<a href="{% url 'create_blog_post' %}">Create a
new blog post</a>
```

This will create a link to the `create_blog_post` view where users can create new blog posts.

Summary

In this chapter, we explored Django's URL routing system and how it maps user requests to views. We learned how to define **URL patterns** and how to use **path converters** to create dynamic URLs. We also covered how to create URLs using **regular expressions** for more complex patterns.

We built a real-world blog application with URL patterns for displaying a list of blog posts, viewing individual blog posts, and creating new ones. This setup demonstrates how Django's URL routing system helps manage user requests and how URLs can be mapped to specific views in a clean and readable way.

In the next chapter, we'll dive deeper into Django forms and handling user input, validating data, and processing form submissions efficiently.

CHAPTER 8

FORMS AND HANDLING USER INPUT

Working with Django Forms

In web applications, forms are one of the most common ways to collect data from users. Django provides an easy-to-use form handling system, which allows you to define forms as Python classes and automatically handle rendering the HTML, validating user input, and processing the form data. Django's **forms** are powerful tools for handling user input in a secure and structured way.

To create a form in Django, you use Django's `forms.Form` class or `forms.ModelForm` for model-backed forms. Here's an overview of both types:

- **forms.Form**: Used when you want to create a form that does not directly correspond to a model in the database.
- **forms.ModelForm**: Used when you want to create a form that is directly tied to a Django model, so it automatically generates form fields based on the model's fields.

A basic Django form is created by subclassing `forms.Form` and adding fields as class attributes. Here's an example of a simple contact form:

```python
# forms.py

from django import forms

class ContactForm(forms.Form):
    name = forms.CharField(max_length=100)
    email = forms.EmailField()
    message                          =
forms.CharField(widget=forms.Textarea)
```

In this example:

- `name`, `email`, and `message` are form fields that will be rendered as input fields in the HTML form.
- The `CharField` is used for text input, and the `EmailField` is used for validating email input.
- `widget=forms.Textarea` makes the `message` field render as a large text area instead of a single-line input.

To render this form in a template, you would simply pass the form instance from your view to the template.

Form Validation, Security, and Error Handling

Django provides a built-in validation mechanism that ensures user input is correct and safe. Here's an overview of how form validation and error handling work in Django:

Form Validation

Django automatically validates form fields based on the field types defined in the form class. For example:

- The CharField will validate that the input is a string.
- The EmailField will check that the input is a valid email address format.
- If a required field is missing, Django will show a validation error.

You can also add custom validation to fields by defining a clean_<field_name> method. Here's an example of a custom validation for the email field:

python

```
# forms.py
```

```python
from django import forms

class ContactForm(forms.Form):
    name = forms.CharField(max_length=100)
    email = forms.EmailField()
    message                                 =
forms.CharField(widget=forms.Textarea)

    def clean_email(self):
        email = self.cleaned_data['email']
        if "example.com" in email:
            raise forms.ValidationError("We  do
not accept emails from example.com")
        return email
```

In this example:

- clean_email() is a custom validation method that checks if the email contains "example.com" and raises a ValidationError if it does.

Error Handling

Django forms automatically handle errors and provide easy access to them in the template. When a form is submitted, Django will check if the form is valid using the is_valid() method. If the form is valid, the data is processed; otherwise, errors are displayed to the user.

In your view, you can check if the form is valid and then handle the errors accordingly:

```python
# views.py

from django.shortcuts import render
from .forms import ContactForm

def contact_view(request):
    if request.method == 'POST':
        form = ContactForm(request.POST)
        if form.is_valid():
            # Process the form data (e.g., send an email, save to the database, etc.)
            # For now, we'll just send a success message
            return render(request, 'contact_success.html')
        else:
            # If the form is invalid, render the form again with errors
            return render(request, 'contact.html', {'form': form})
    else:
        form = ContactForm()
        return render(request, 'contact.html', {'form': form})
```

In the above view:

- If the form is valid (`form.is_valid()`), we process the form and send the user to a success page.
- If the form is invalid, we re-render the form, including any validation errors.

Displaying Errors in Templates

Django provides easy access to form errors in the template. If a form has errors, they will be available through the `form.errors` attribute. You can display these errors in the HTML like this:

html

```html
<!-- contact.html -->

<form method="post">
    {% csrf_token %}
    {{ form.as_p }}

    {% if form.errors %}
        <ul>
            {% for field in form %}
                {% for error in field.errors %}
                    <li>{{ error }}</li>
                {% endfor %}
            {% endfor %}
        </ul>
```

87

```
{% endif %}
<button type="submit">Submit</button>
</form>
```

In this template:

- `{{ form.as_p }}` automatically renders the form fields with appropriate HTML markup (each field is rendered inside a `<p>` tag).
- The `{% if form.errors %}` block checks if there are any validation errors, and then displays each error message in a list.

Security Considerations

When working with forms in Django, security is a top priority. Django automatically protects your forms from several common security vulnerabilities:

- **Cross-Site Request Forgery (CSRF)**: Django uses a CSRF token to protect against CSRF attacks. This token is added to every form automatically using `{% csrf_token %}` in the template.
- **Cross-Site Scripting (XSS)**: Django automatically escapes user input in templates, preventing XSS attacks where a malicious user could inject JavaScript into your page.

Real-World Example: Creating and Handling Contact Forms

Let's create a **contact form** for a blog app. This form will collect the user's name, email, and message. After the form is submitted, we'll process the data and send a confirmation message.

Step 1: Define the Form

Here's the form definition for the contact form:

```python
# forms.py

from django import forms

class ContactForm(forms.Form):
    name    =    forms.CharField(max_length=100,
required=True)
    email = forms.EmailField(required=True)
    message                                    =
forms.CharField(widget=forms.Textarea,
required=True)
```

Step 2: Define the View

In `views.py`, we will handle the form submission and validate the data:

```python
python

# views.py

from django.shortcuts import render
from .forms import ContactForm

def contact_view(request):
    if request.method == 'POST':
        form = ContactForm(request.POST)
        if form.is_valid():
            # Process the form (for example,
sending an email or saving to the database)
            # Here, we'll just render a success
message
            return          render(request,
'contact_success.html')
        else:
            # If the form is invalid, render the
form again with errors
            return          render(request,
'contact.html', {'form': form})
    else:
        form = ContactForm()
        return  render(request,  'contact.html',
{'form': form})
```

Step 3: Define the URL

In `urls.py`, we'll define the URL pattern for the contact form page:

```
python
```

```python
# urls.py

from django.urls import path
from . import views

urlpatterns = [
    path('contact/',        views.contact_view,
name='contact'),
]
```

Step 4: Create the Template

Now, let's create the `contact.html` template for displaying the form:

```
html
```

```html
<!-- contact.html -->

{% extends "base.html" %}

{% block title %}Contact Us{% endblock %}
```

```
{% block content %}
  <h1>Contact Us</h1>

  <form method="post">
    {% csrf_token %}
    {{ form.as_p }}

    {% if form.errors %}
      <ul>
        {% for field in form %}
          {% for error in field.errors %}
            <li>{{ error }}</li>
          {% endfor %}
        {% endfor %}
      </ul>
    {% endif %}

    <button type="submit">Submit</button>
  </form>
{% endblock %}
```

In this template:

- We use `{{ form.as_p }}` to render the form fields.
- If there are any form errors, they will be displayed as a list under the form fields.

Step 5: Create the Success Page

Once the form is submitted successfully, we'll display a success message:

html

```
<!-- contact_success.html -->

{% extends "base.html" %}

{% block title %}Thank You!{% endblock %}

{% block content %}
  <h1>Thank you for contacting us!</h1>
  <p>Your message has been received. We will get
back to you shortly.</p>
{% endblock %}
```

Summary

In this chapter, we explored how to work with forms in Django, including form validation, security, and error handling. We covered how to create forms using both `forms.Form` and `forms.ModelForm`, validated form data, and displayed error messages in the templates.

We then built a **real-world contact form** that collects the user's name, email, and message, processes the form submission, and displays a success message. This demonstrates how Django simplifies the process of handling user input securely and efficiently.

In the next chapter, we'll learn about **model forms** and how to create forms directly tied to Django models, allowing for easier management of database records.

CHAPTER 9

USER AUTHENTICATION AND AUTHORIZATION

Django's Authentication System Explained

User authentication and authorization are critical components of any web application. **Authentication** verifies the identity of users, while **authorization** ensures that users can only access the resources and actions they are permitted to.

Django provides a built-in **authentication system** that handles common tasks like user registration, login, logout, password management, and more. This system is robust, secure, and highly customizable.

Django's authentication system uses the following core components:

- **User Model**: Represents the user in the system. By default, Django provides a `User` model that stores basic information such as username, password, email, and user-related metadata (e.g., first and last name).
- **Authentication Backend**: Responsible for verifying the user's credentials (e.g., checking if the entered password matches the one stored in the database).

- **Authentication Views**: Django provides pre-built views for handling login, logout, and password management, which you can customize as needed.

- **Session Management**: Once a user is authenticated, Django creates a session to track their logged-in state across different requests.

- **Permissions and Groups**: Django allows you to define custom permissions and groups to manage user access to specific resources.

Django's authentication system is designed to be flexible and extensible. You can easily override default behavior, customize user models, and add new authentication methods if needed.

Managing User Registration, Login, and Logout

User Registration

Django does not provide a built-in registration view out of the box, but you can easily create one. Registration typically involves creating a form for users to enter their details (e.g., username, email, password), validating the data, and creating a new `User` object if everything is correct.

Here's an example of a basic user registration form:

```python
```

```python
# forms.py

from django import forms
from django.contrib.auth.models import User
from        django.core.exceptions        import
ValidationError

class RegistrationForm(forms.Form):
    username = forms.CharField(max_length=100)
    email = forms.EmailField()
    password                                      =
forms.CharField(widget=forms.PasswordInput())
    password_confirm                              =
forms.CharField(widget=forms.PasswordInput())

    def clean_password_confirm(self):
        password                                  =
self.cleaned_data.get('password')
        password_confirm                          =
self.cleaned_data.get('password_confirm')
        if password != password_confirm:
            raise  ValidationError("Passwords  do
not match")
        return password_confirm

    def save(self):
        user = User.objects.create_user(

username=self.cleaned_data['username'],
```

```
        email=self.cleaned_data['email'],

password=self.cleaned_data['password']
        )
        return user
```

In this form:

- We validate that the two password fields match using the `clean_password_confirm` method.
- If the form is valid, we create a new user using Django's `create_user` method, which ensures the password is hashed before being stored.

In your `views.py`, you would handle the form submission and create the user:

python

```
# views.py

from django.shortcuts import render, redirect
from .forms import RegistrationForm

def register(request):
    if request.method == 'POST':
        form = RegistrationForm(request.POST)
        if form.is_valid():
            form.save()
```

```
            return redirect('login')  # Redirect
to login page after successful registration
    else:
        form = RegistrationForm()

    return     render(request,    'register.html',
{'form': form})
```

Here, we handle both GET and POST requests. On POST, we validate the form and create a new user if the form is valid. After registration, the user is redirected to the login page.

User Login

Django provides a built-in login system that you can use to authenticate users. You can use the LoginView class from django.contrib.auth.views to handle user login.

Here's how you can implement the login functionality:

python

```
# urls.py

from django.contrib.auth.views import LoginView
from django.urls import path

urlpatterns = [
```

```
    path('login/',              LoginView.as_view(),
name='login'),
]
```

In your template, you can render the login form as follows:

```html
<!-- login.html -->

<form method="post">
    {% csrf_token %}
    {{ form.as_p }}
    <button type="submit">Login</button>
</form>
```

Django automatically provides a `login.html` form, but you can customize it to meet your needs.

User Logout

To log out users, Django provides the `LogoutView` class, which is also part of `django.contrib.auth.views`. You can add a logout URL to your `urls.py`:

```python
# urls.py

from django.contrib.auth.views import LogoutView
```

```
from django.urls import path

urlpatterns = [
    path('logout/',          LogoutView.as_view(),
name='logout'),
]
```

When a user accesses the `logout/` URL, Django logs them out and redirects them to the homepage (or any other URL you specify).

Permissions and Roles: Handling User Access

Django allows you to manage permissions and restrict access to specific views based on the user's role or permissions. This is useful for applications where different users have different levels of access.

Permissions

Django has a built-in permissions system that allows you to define what actions a user can perform on specific models. Permissions are created automatically for each model (e.g., `add_blogpost`, `change_blogpost`, `delete_blogpost`).

You can check a user's permissions in views or templates using the `has_perm` method:

```python
# views.py

from django.shortcuts import render
from django.contrib.auth.decorators import permission_required

@permission_required('blog.add_blogpost', raise_exception=True)
def create_blog_post(request):
    return render(request, 'create_blog_post.html')
```

In this example, the `create_blog_post` view will only be accessible to users who have the `add_blogpost` permission.

Groups

Django also provides **groups**, which are a way of managing permissions for multiple users at once. For example, you can create a group called "Editors" and give them permissions to add and edit blog posts. When you assign a user to the "Editors" group, they automatically inherit the permissions assigned to that group.

You can manage groups and permissions in the Django admin panel, or you can assign groups programmatically using the `Group` model:

```python
python

from django.contrib.auth.models import Group

# Create a new group and assign permissions
editors_group                              =
Group.objects.create(name='Editors')
editors_group.permissions.add(permission_to_add
_blogpost)
```

You can then assign users to this group:

```python
python

# Assign a user to the Editors group
user.groups.add(editors_group)
```

Restricting Access to Views

To restrict access to views based on user roles or permissions, you can use Django's `user_passes_test` decorator or the `LoginRequiredMixin` for class-based views.

For function-based views, you can use the `login_required` decorator to ensure that only authenticated users can access a view:

```python
python
```

```
from     django.contrib.auth.decorators     import
login_required

@login_required
def create_blog_post(request):
    return                      render(request,
'create_blog_post.html')
```

For class-based views, you can use the `LoginRequiredMixin`
to enforce login for a specific view:

```
python
```

```
from     django.contrib.auth.mixins     import
LoginRequiredMixin
from django.views.generic import TemplateView

class     CreateBlogPostView(LoginRequiredMixin,
TemplateView):
    template_name = 'create_blog_post.html'
```

This ensures that only authenticated users can access the view, and
if an unauthenticated user attempts to access the view, they will
be redirected to the login page.

Real-World Example: Implementing a User Login System for Your Blog

Let's implement a user login system for your blog app. We'll allow users to register, log in, log out, and view their profile after authentication.

Step 1: Define the Registration and Login Views

We already defined the registration and login views earlier in this chapter. The registration view handles user sign-up, while Django's built-in `LoginView` handles logging users in.

Step 2: Create Templates for Registration, Login, and Logout

1. **Registration Template (`register.html`):**

html

```
<!-- register.html -->

<form method="post">
    {% csrf_token %}
    {{ form.as_p }}
    <button type="submit">Register</button>
</form>
```

2. **Login Template (`login.html`):**

html

```
<!-- login.html -->

<form method="post">
    {% csrf_token %}
    {{ form.as_p }}
    <button type="submit">Login</button>
</form>
```

3. **Logout Template (logout.html):**

html

```
<!-- logout.html -->

<p>You have successfully logged out. <a href="{%
url 'login' %}">Login again</a>.</p>
```

Step 3: Restrict Access to the Blog Creation Page

We can restrict access to the blog creation page to only authenticated users by using the login_required decorator:

python

```
# views.py

from    django.contrib.auth.decorators    import
login_required
```

```
@login_required
def create_blog_post(request):
    # Your blog post creation logic here
    return                      render(request,
'create_blog_post.html')
```

This ensures that only logged-in users can access the page.

Summary

In this chapter, we explored Django's **authentication and authorization system**. We discussed how to manage **user registration, login, and logout**, as well as how to handle **permissions and roles** to control user access to different parts of the application.

We implemented a **user login system** for a blog app, allowing users to register, log in, and access certain pages based on their authentication status. Django's built-in authentication tools, such as the `LoginView` and `LogoutView`, simplify the process of adding user authentication to your app.

In the next chapter, we will dive deeper into **working with static and media files** in Django, ensuring that your application handles CSS, JavaScript, images, and user-uploaded files efficiently.

CHAPTER 10

HANDLING STATIC FILES AND MEDIA FILES

Understanding Static Files and Media in Django

In Django, **static files** and **media files** refer to two types of content that are served by your web application. While both are used for handling non-dynamic content, they serve different purposes:

- **Static files**: These are files that do not change and are used for rendering your website's frontend. Examples of static files include:
    - **CSS files**: Used for styling the layout and appearance of the web page.
    - **JavaScript files**: Used for adding interactivity to the page, such as form validation or dynamic content loading.
    - **Images**: Used for logos, icons, and other fixed visual content.
- **Media files**: These are user-uploaded files that are dynamically generated or modified. For example:
    - User profile pictures
    - Uploaded documents

o Blog images (or any other files uploaded by the user)

Django has a built-in system to manage both static and media files. **Static files** are usually handled during development and are served by Django automatically, while **media files** (user-uploaded content) are managed through Django's file storage system.

Serving CSS, JavaScript, and Image Files

Static Files Configuration

Django provides a simple way to manage static files by keeping them separate from dynamic content. During development, Django automatically serves static files using the `django.contrib.staticfiles` app. In production, you would configure a web server (e.g., Nginx or Apache) to serve static files more efficiently.

Step 1: Setting Up Static Files in Django

In your Django settings (`settings.py`), define the following settings for static files:

```python
python
```

```python
# settings.py
```

```
# URL to access static files in the browser
STATIC_URL = '/static/'

# Directory where static files are stored
STATICFILES_DIRS = [
    BASE_DIR / 'static',
]

# The directory where collected static files will
be stored during deployment
STATIC_ROOT = BASE_DIR / 'staticfiles'
```

- **STATIC_URL**: This is the URL where static files will be accessible in the browser.
- **STATICFILES_DIRS**: This is a list of directories where Django will search for static files. You can place static files (like CSS and JavaScript) inside a static/ folder in your app directory or in a global static/ folder.
- **STATIC_ROOT**: This is the directory where static files will be collected when you run the collectstatic command. This is used in production for serving static files.

Step 2: Organizing Static Files

Django expects static files to be placed in specific directories. Here's how you can organize them:

1. **In your app directory**:
   - Create a `static/` directory inside your Django app (e.g., `blog/static/`).
   - Inside the `static/` directory, create subdirectories for CSS, JavaScript, and images:

   ```cpp
   blog/
     static/
       css/
         style.css
       js/
         script.js
       images/
         logo.png
   ```

2. **Global static files**:
   - You can also store global static files outside of your apps. This is useful for shared assets like site-wide CSS or JavaScript files.

Step 3: Linking Static Files in Templates

To use static files in your Django templates, you need to load them with the `{% static %}` template tag. First, ensure that you load the static files at the top of your template:

```html
```

```
{% load static %}
```

Then, you can reference static files like CSS, JavaScript, and images using the {% static %} tag:

```html
<!-- Linking CSS -->
<link rel="stylesheet" type="text/css" href="{%
static 'css/style.css' %}">

<!-- Linking JavaScript -->
<script src="{% static 'js/script.js'
%}"></script>

<!-- Displaying an image -->
<img src="{% static 'images/logo.png' %}"
alt="Logo">
```

Django will automatically resolve the correct path to the static files, whether you're in development or production.

Step 4: Collecting Static Files for Production

In production, Django doesn't serve static files directly; instead, you use the collectstatic command to gather all static files into a single location for a web server (e.g., Nginx) to serve efficiently.

To collect static files, run:

```bash
```

```
python manage.py collectstatic
```

This command will gather all static files from each app and place them in the directory defined by STATIC_ROOT.

Media Files in Django

Media files are files that users upload, such as images, documents, and other user-generated content. Django handles media files by storing them in a specified directory and allowing users to upload files through forms.

Step 1: Configure Media Files in Django

In your settings.py file, define the following settings for media files:

```python
# settings.py

# URL to access media files in the browser
MEDIA_URL = '/media/'
```

```
# Directory where uploaded media files will be
stored
MEDIA_ROOT = BASE_DIR / 'media'
```

- **MEDIA_URL**: The URL where users can access media files.
- **MEDIA_ROOT**: The directory where media files are stored on the server.

Step 2: Handling File Uploads in Forms

To allow users to upload files, you need to create a form with a `FileField` or `ImageField`:

python

```
# forms.py

from django import forms

class ProfileForm(forms.Form):
    profile_picture = forms.ImageField()
```

This form allows users to upload an image, which will be saved in the `MEDIA_ROOT` directory.

In your view, you would handle the file upload like this:

python

```python
# views.py

from django.shortcuts import render
from .forms import ProfileForm

def profile_view(request):
    if request.method == 'POST':
        form        =        ProfileForm(request.POST,
request.FILES)
        if form.is_valid():
            # Process the form data and save the
file
            form.save()   # In case you're using
a model form
            return                 render(request,
'profile_success.html')
    else:
        form = ProfileForm()

    return     render(request,     'profile.html',
{'form': form})
```

- The `request.FILES` object is used to access the uploaded files.
- Django will automatically store the uploaded file in the directory specified by `MEDIA_ROOT`.

Step 3: Displaying Media Files in Templates

To display media files (such as images uploaded by users), use the MEDIA_URL setting. Here's how to display an uploaded image in a template:

html

```
<!-- profile.html -->

{% if user.profile_picture %}
    <img src="{{ user.profile_picture.url }}"
alt="Profile Picture">
{% else %}
    <p>No profile picture uploaded.</p>
{% endif %}
```

In this template:

- user.profile_picture.url is the URL to the media file stored in the database.
- Django automatically generates the correct URL to serve the media file based on the MEDIA_URL setting.

Step 4: Serving Media Files in Development

In development, Django automatically serves media files. You need to add the following to your urls.py to enable serving media files during development:

```python
# urls.py

from django.conf import settings
from django.conf.urls.static import static
from django.urls import path
from . import views

urlpatterns = [
    path('profile/',            views.profile_view,
name='profile'),
]

# Serve media files during development
if settings.DEBUG:
    urlpatterns += static(settings.MEDIA_URL,
document_root=settings.MEDIA_ROOT)
```

This setup allows you to serve media files when DEBUG is set to True. In production, a web server like Nginx or Apache should serve media files more efficiently.

Real-World Example: Adding Media Files to Your Blog App

Let's apply everything we've learned by adding media files to your blog app. We will allow users to upload an image for their blog posts and display it on the blog detail page.

Step 1: Modify the BlogPost Model

First, update the `BlogPost` model to include an image field:

python

```python
# models.py

from django.db import models

class BlogPost(models.Model):
    title = models.CharField(max_length=200)
    content = models.TextField()
    created_at                        =
models.DateTimeField(auto_now_add=True)
    image                             =
models.ImageField(upload_to='blog_images/',
null=True, blank=True)

    def __str__(self):
        return self.title
```

In this example:

- We add an `image` field to the `BlogPost` model, which allows users to upload images for each post.
- The `upload_to='blog_images/'` argument specifies that the images should be saved in the `media/blog_images/` directory.

118

Step 2: Modify the Form to Handle Image Uploads

In `forms.py`, add an `ImageField` to the `BlogPostForm`:

python

```
# forms.py

from django import forms
from .models import BlogPost

class BlogPostForm(forms.ModelForm):
    class Meta:
        model = BlogPost
        fields = ['title', 'content', 'image']
```

This form will now allow users to upload an image when creating or editing a blog post.

Step 3: Modify the View to Handle File Uploads

In `views.py`, ensure that the POST request includes the uploaded file:

python

```
# views.py

from django.shortcuts import render, redirect
from .forms import BlogPostForm
```

```
def create_blog_post(request):
    if request.method == 'POST':
        form    =    BlogPostForm(request.POST,
request.FILES)
        if form.is_valid():
            form.save()
            return redirect('blog_home')
    else:
        form = BlogPostForm()
    return                    render(request,
'create_blog_post.html', {'form': form})
```

We pass `request.FILES` along with `request.POST` to handle file uploads.

Step 4: Displaying the Uploaded Image in the Blog Detail Page

Finally, modify the `blog_detail.html` template to display the image:

html

```
<!-- blog_detail.html -->

<h1>{{ post.title }}</h1>
<p>{{ post.content }}</p>
{% if post.image %}
```

```
<img src="{{ post.image.url }}" alt="Blog
Post Image">
{% endif %}
```

This will display the image uploaded by the user for each blog post.

Summary

In this chapter, we explored how to handle **static files** (like CSS, JavaScript, and images) and **media files** (like user-uploaded images) in Django. We learned how to:

- Configure Django to serve static files during development.
- Set up STATIC_URL and MEDIA_URL to manage static and media files.
- Use **ImageField** for handling user-uploaded images and display them in templates.
- Use collectstatic for collecting static files in preparation for production deployment.

We also implemented a **real-world example** of adding media files to your blog app, allowing users to upload images for blog posts and display them on the blog detail page.

In the next chapter, we will dive into **Django's admin interface**, which allows you to manage your application's data using a web-based interface.

CHAPTER 11

DJANGO ADMIN INTERFACE: MANAGING CONTENT

Introduction to Django's Built-in Admin Panel

One of Django's most powerful features is its built-in **admin interface**. This feature allows developers and site administrators to manage application data directly from a web-based interface without needing to interact with the database or write custom interfaces.

The **Django admin** is automatically generated for any model you define in your application, providing an intuitive and powerful way to create, edit, and delete records. It's built using Django's ORM and dynamically generates the admin interface for your models, making it an invaluable tool for content management.

By default, the admin panel allows you to perform CRUD (Create, Read, Update, Delete) operations on models. For example, you can easily add, modify, or delete blog posts, user profiles, or any other content stored in your database.

To use the Django admin interface, you need to:

1. Create a superuser account (if you haven't done so already).
2. Register your models with the admin panel.
3. Customize the admin interface as needed.

Customizing the Admin Interface

While Django's default admin interface works out of the box, it's often beneficial to customize it to fit the needs of your project. Customizations might include things like:

- Changing how model fields are displayed.
- Adding search or filter functionality.
- Grouping related fields in a more user-friendly way.

Step 1: Create a Superuser Account

To access the Django admin interface, you first need to create a superuser account, which is a special user with admin privileges.

To create a superuser, run the following command:

```bash
```

```
python manage.py createsuperuser
```

You'll be prompted to provide a username, email, and password. After creating the superuser, you can access the admin interface by visiting:

```arduino
```

```
http://127.0.0.1:8000/admin/
```

Log in using the superuser credentials you just created.

Step 2: Registering Models with the Admin Panel

By default, models are not available in the admin interface. To make them accessible, you need to register your models with the admin panel. This is done in the admin.py file within your app directory.

Here's how you can register a BlogPost model to appear in the admin interface:

```python
```

```python
# admin.py

from django.contrib import admin
from .models import BlogPost

# Registering the BlogPost model with the admin
interface
```

```
admin.site.register(BlogPost)
```

Once you've registered the model, you can access and manage the BlogPost entries through the admin panel.

Step 3: Customizing the Admin Interface

Django allows you to customize how models appear in the admin interface. This includes customizing the display of fields, adding search functionality, adding filters, and more.

Here's how you can customize the BlogPost model's admin interface:

```
python

# admin.py

from django.contrib import admin
from .models import BlogPost

class BlogPostAdmin(admin.ModelAdmin):
    list_display = ('title', 'author',
'created_at', 'updated_at')  # Display these
fields in the list view
    search_fields = ('title', 'content')  # Add
search functionality for these fields
    list_filter = ('created_at', 'author') # Add
filters for these fields
```

```
    ordering = ('-created_at',)   # Order blog
posts by creation date in descending order

# Register the customized BlogPostAdmin class
admin.site.register(BlogPost, BlogPostAdmin)
```

Customization Features:

1. **list_display**: This defines which fields will be shown in the list view for this model. In this case, we display the title, author, created_at, and updated_at fields.
2. **search_fields**: This adds a search bar to the admin panel. You can specify which fields should be searchable. In this case, title and content are searchable.
3. **list_filter**: This adds a filter sidebar to the admin interface. You can filter the list of blog posts based on specific fields, such as created_at and author.
4. **ordering**: This controls the default ordering of the objects in the list view. Here, we order the blog posts by created_at in descending order (-created_at).

Step 4: Adding Inline Models to the Admin Panel

If you have related models (e.g., comments on a blog post), you can display them inline within the admin interface. This is useful for managing related data directly from the parent model.

127

For example, let's say each BlogPost has multiple Comment entries. You can add Comment as an inline model inside the BlogPost admin interface:

python

```
# admin.py

from django.contrib import admin
from .models import BlogPost, Comment

class CommentInline(admin.TabularInline):    #
Using TabularInline to display comments in a
table-like format
    model = Comment
    extra = 1  # Number of empty forms to display
initially

class BlogPostAdmin(admin.ModelAdmin):
    list_display    =    ('title',    'author',
'created_at', 'updated_at')
    search_fields = ('title', 'content')
    list_filter = ('created_at', 'author')
    ordering = ('-created_at',)
    inlines = [CommentInline]    # Adding the
CommentInline to the BlogPostAdmin

admin.site.register(BlogPost, BlogPostAdmin)
```

In this example:

- `CommentInline` is an inline model that will display the comments associated with each blog post directly in the blog post edit page.
- `extra = 1` specifies that one empty form for a new comment will be displayed by default.

Step 5: Customizing the Admin Form for a Model

Sometimes, you may want to customize the form used for adding or editing a model in the admin interface. You can do this using `ModelAdmin`'s `fieldsets` or `fields` attributes.

For example, let's customize the form for creating or editing a `BlogPost` to organize the fields into sections:

python

```
# admin.py

from django.contrib import admin
from .models import BlogPost

class BlogPostAdmin(admin.ModelAdmin):
    list_display = ('title', 'author',
'created_at', 'updated_at')
    search_fields = ('title', 'content')
    list_filter = ('created_at', 'author')
```

129

```
    ordering = ('-created_at',)
    fieldsets = (
        (None, {
            'fields': ('title', 'content')
        }),
        ('Metadata', {
            'classes': ('collapse',),
            'fields': ('author', 'created_at',
'updated_at')
        }),
    )  # Customizing the form layout
```

```
admin.site.register(BlogPost, BlogPostAdmin)
```

In this example:

- We use `fieldsets` to organize the form into two sections: one for the main fields (`title`, `content`) and one for metadata (`author`, `created_at`, `updated_at`).
- The `classes` option adds a "collapse" class to the "Metadata" section, making it collapsible in the admin interface.

Real-World Example: Admin Dashboard for Managing Blog Posts

Let's implement a full admin dashboard for managing blog posts in a blog app. We'll make the following customizations:

1. Display blog posts in a table with columns for `title`, `author`, `created_at`, and `updated_at`.
2. Add the ability to search and filter blog posts.
3. Include inline editing for comments related to each blog post.

Step 1: Define the Models

Let's start with the `BlogPost` and `Comment` models:

python

```
# models.py

from django.db import models

class BlogPost(models.Model):
    title = models.CharField(max_length=200)
    content = models.TextField()
    author = models.CharField(max_length=100)
    created_at                                   =
models.DateTimeField(auto_now_add=True)
    updated_at                                   =
models.DateTimeField(auto_now=True)

    def __str__(self):
        return self.title

class Comment(models.Model):
```

131

```
    blog_post    =    models.ForeignKey(BlogPost,
related_name="comments",
on_delete=models.CASCADE)
    author = models.CharField(max_length=100)
    content = models.TextField()
    created_at                            =
models.DateTimeField(auto_now_add=True)

    def __str__(self):
        return  f"Comment  by  {self.author}  on
{self.blog_post.title}"
```

In this example, we have two models:

- `BlogPost`: Stores blog posts, with fields for the title, content, author, and timestamps.
- `Comment`: Stores comments associated with each blog post, with fields for the author, content, and timestamp.

Step 2: Register the Models in the Admin Panel

Now, let's register the `BlogPost` and `Comment` models in `admin.py`:

python

```
# admin.py

from django.contrib import admin
```

```
from .models import BlogPost, Comment

class CommentInline(admin.TabularInline):
    model = Comment
    extra = 1

class BlogPostAdmin(admin.ModelAdmin):
    list_display   =   ('title',   'author',
'created_at', 'updated_at')
    search_fields = ('title', 'content')
    list_filter = ('created_at', 'author')
    ordering = ('-created_at',)
    inlines = [CommentInline]

admin.site.register(BlogPost, BlogPostAdmin)
admin.site.register(Comment)
```

In this admin setup:

- The `CommentInline` is used to display related comments in the blog post edit page.
- The `BlogPostAdmin` class customizes the list view to display `title`, `author`, `created_at`, and `updated_at` in a table, adds search functionality, and provides filtering options.

Step 3: Access the Admin Panel

Once you've made these changes, you can log in to the admin panel and manage your blog posts and comments directly:

- You can view and edit the list of blog posts, search and filter them, and even add or edit comments inline.
- You can easily navigate the admin interface to create, update, or delete blog posts and comments.

Summary

In this chapter, we explored **Django's built-in admin interface** and how it can be used to manage content in your application. We learned how to:

- Register models with the admin interface.
- Customize the admin interface using `ModelAdmin` options like `list_display`, `search_fields`, and `list_filter`.
- Use **inline models** for related objects like comments.
- Customize the form layout for models using `fieldsets`.
- Implement a real-world **admin dashboard** for managing blog posts and comments.

The Django admin interface is a powerful tool for managing application content with minimal effort, and its flexibility allows you to customize it to fit the needs of your project.

In the next chapter, we'll dive into **testing Django applications**, learning how to write unit tests to ensure the reliability of your web app.

CHAPTER 12

WORKING WITH DJANGO'S ORM: ADVANCED QUERIES

Advanced Querying Techniques in Django ORM

Django's **Object-Relational Mapping (ORM)** allows you to interact with the database using Python code instead of raw SQL queries. While the ORM simplifies most database operations, it also offers advanced querying techniques that allow you to perform complex queries, aggregate data, and join related models. In this chapter, we'll explore some of these advanced techniques, including filtering, aggregation, and performing joins.

1. Filtering Data with Django ORM

Filtering data in Django's ORM is done using the `filter()` method. The `filter()` method allows you to specify conditions that records must satisfy to be included in the query results.

For example, let's say you want to retrieve all blog posts created by a specific author:

```python
```

```
# Fetch all blog posts by a specific author
```

```
posts_by_author                                    =
BlogPost.objects.filter(author="John Doe")
```

You can use various query operators in the `filter()` method:

- **Exact match**: `field=value`
- **Case-insensitive match**: `field__iexact=value`
- **Contains**: `field__contains=value`
- **Greater than or less than**: `field__gt=value`, `field__lt=value`
- **Date range**: `field__gte=value`, `field__lte=value`

For example, to find blog posts containing the word "Python" in their content, use the `contains` filter:

```python
# Fetch all blog posts with the word 'Python' in
the content
python_posts                                       =
BlogPost.objects.filter(content__contains="Pyth
on")
```

2. Using Aggregates to Summarize Data

Django allows you to perform aggregation operations to summarize or compute values over a set of data. Aggregates are useful when you need to calculate things like totals, averages, counts, and more.

To perform aggregation, you can use the `aggregate()` function, which computes values across the queryset.

Here's an example of counting the total number of blog posts and calculating the average word count of blog posts:

```python
from django.db.models import Count, Avg

# Count the number of blog posts
post_count                                      =
BlogPost.objects.aggregate(post_count=Count('id
'))

# Calculate the average length of blog posts
avg_post_length                                 =
BlogPost.objects.aggregate(avg_length=Avg('cont
ent'))

print(post_count)  # Output: {'post_count': 100}
print(avg_post_length)  # Output: {'avg_length':
250.5}
```

You can use several built-in aggregate functions in Django:

- **Count**: Returns the number of objects
- **Avg**: Returns the average value of a field
- **Sum**: Returns the total sum of a field
- **Max** and **Min**: Return the maximum or minimum value of a field

3. Using Joins to Combine Related Models

Django's ORM also supports **joins** to combine data from related models. When models are related through foreign keys, you can easily query across related models using **select_related** (for single-valued relationships) and **prefetch_related** (for multi-valued relationships).

Using `select_related` for ForeignKey Relationships

The `select_related` method performs a SQL join and retrieves related objects in a single query, which is more efficient when you have a **one-to-one** or **many-to-one** relationship.

For example, let's say we have a `BlogPost` model that has a foreign key to an `Author` model. To retrieve blog posts along with their associated author in one query, you can use `select_related`:

python

```python
# Fetch blog posts with the related author in one
query
posts_with_author                              =
BlogPost.objects.select_related('author').all()

for post in posts_with_author:
    print(post.title, post.author.name)
```

This minimizes the number of queries to the database because Django uses a single query to retrieve the blog posts and their corresponding authors.

Using `prefetch_related` for Many-to-Many and Reverse ForeignKey Relationships

The `prefetch_related` method is used for **many-to-many** and **reverse foreign key** relationships. Unlike `select_related`, which works for single-valued relationships, `prefetch_related` performs separate queries and then combines the results in Python.

For example, to retrieve all blog posts with their related tags (many-to-many relationship), you can use `prefetch_related`:

```python
python
```

```python
# Fetch all blog posts with their related tags
posts_with_tags                              =
BlogPost.objects.prefetch_related('tags').all()
```

```
for post in posts_with_tags:
    print(post.title,    [tag.name    for    tag    in
post.tags.all()])
```

In this example, Django performs two queries: one to get the blog posts and one to get the tags related to each post. It then combines the results in Python.

Real-World Example: Filtering Blog Posts by Category and Tags

Let's build a real-world example of filtering blog posts based on categories and tags.

Step 1: Define the Models

We'll define three models:

1. **Category**: A category for organizing blog posts (e.g., "Technology", "Lifestyle").
2. **Tag**: Tags that can be associated with blog posts (e.g., "Python", "Django").
3. **BlogPost**: The main blog post model that includes a foreign key to `Category` and a many-to-many relationship with `Tag`.

```python
```

```python
# models.py

from django.db import models

class Category(models.Model):
    name = models.CharField(max_length=100)

    def __str__(self):
        return self.name

class Tag(models.Model):
    name = models.CharField(max_length=50)

    def __str__(self):
        return self.name

class BlogPost(models.Model):
    title = models.CharField(max_length=200)
    content = models.TextField()
    category    =    models.ForeignKey(Category,
on_delete=models.CASCADE)
    tags    =    models.ManyToManyField(Tag,
related_name='blog_posts')
    created_at                            =
models.DateTimeField(auto_now_add=True)

    def __str__(self):
        return self.title
```

In this example:

- Category stores the category of each blog post (e.g., "Technology", "Lifestyle").
- Tag stores tags that can be associated with blog posts (e.g., "Python", "Django").
- BlogPost includes a foreign key to Category and a many-to-many relationship with Tag.

Step 2: Querying Blog Posts by Category and Tags

Now let's write a query to filter blog posts by category and tags.

Filtering by Category: To retrieve all blog posts in the "Technology" category, we can use the filter() method:

```python
# Fetch blog posts in the 'Technology' category
technology_category = Category.objects.get(name='Technology')
tech_posts = BlogPost.objects.filter(category=technology_category)

for post in tech_posts:
    print(post.title)
```

Filtering by Tags: To filter blog posts that are tagged with a specific tag (e.g., "Python"), we can use filter() on the tags related manager:

```python

# Fetch blog posts with the 'Python' tag
python_tag = Tag.objects.get(name='Python')
python_posts                                =
BlogPost.objects.filter(tags=python_tag)

for post in python_posts:
    print(post.title)
```

Combining Filters for Category and Tags: You can combine filters to narrow down results. For example, to find blog posts in the "Technology" category that are tagged with "Python", you can use the following query:

```python

# Fetch blog posts in the 'Technology' category
and tagged with 'Python'
python_tag = Tag.objects.get(name='Python')
technology_category                         =
Category.objects.get(name='Technology')

filtered_posts                              =
BlogPost.objects.filter(category=technology_cat
egory, tags=python_tag)

for post in filtered_posts:
    print(post.title)
```

144

This query will return blog posts that belong to the "Technology" category and are tagged with "Python".

Summary

In this chapter, we explored advanced querying techniques in Django's ORM. We covered:

- **Filtering**: Using `filter()` to retrieve data based on specific conditions, such as matching exact values, performing range queries, or searching text fields.
- **Aggregation**: Using `aggregate()` to calculate totals, averages, and other summary statistics on a set of data.
- **Joins**: Using `select_related` and `prefetch_related` to perform efficient joins and fetch related data in a single or optimized set of queries.
- **Real-world example**: Filtering blog posts by category and tags using Django's ORM, demonstrating how to combine filters and work with related models.

These advanced querying techniques will help you efficiently interact with your database and retrieve the exact data you need, whether you're building simple or complex queries.

In the next chapter, we'll dive into **Django's signals** and how they can be used to trigger actions when certain events occur in your application.

CHAPTER 13

BUILDING APIS WITH DJANGO REST FRAMEWORK (DRF)

Introduction to Django Rest Framework (DRF)

Django Rest Framework (DRF) is a powerful toolkit for building Web APIs in Django. It provides tools for creating RESTful (Representational State Transfer) APIs quickly and efficiently. A RESTful API allows clients (such as web browsers, mobile apps, or other services) to interact with your application by sending HTTP requests (like GET, POST, PUT, DELETE) and receiving data, typically in JSON format.

DRF offers many benefits:

- **Serialization**: DRF allows you to convert complex data types, like Django models, into JSON (or other formats) that can be easily consumed by clients.
- **Authentication**: DRF supports various authentication methods, such as token-based authentication, session authentication, and OAuth2.
- **Viewsets**: DRF provides `ViewSets`, which simplify the creation of views that handle CRUD operations (Create, Read, Update, Delete) for your models.

147

- **Browsable API**: DRF provides an interactive, browsable web interface that makes it easy to test your API endpoints directly from the browser.

In this chapter, we'll explore how to set up a RESTful API using DRF and build an API for a simple blog app, which will allow clients to interact with the blog posts, retrieve data, and even create new posts.

Setting Up a RESTful API with DRF

Step 1: Install Django Rest Framework (DRF)

To get started, you first need to install DRF. In your project's virtual environment, run the following command:

bash

```
pip install djangorestframework
```

Once DRF is installed, add `'rest_framework'` to the INSTALLED_APPS list in your settings.py:

python

```
# settings.py

INSTALLED_APPS = [
```

```
    # other apps
    'rest_framework',
]
```

Step 2: Create a Serializer

In Django, a **serializer** is used to convert complex data types, like Django model instances, into a format (typically JSON) that can be easily rendered into a response. DRF makes serialization straightforward using `serializers.ModelSerializer`.

Let's create a serializer for the `BlogPost` model, which we defined earlier. This serializer will define how the `BlogPost` model should be converted to and from JSON.

Create a file called `serializers.py`:

python

```python
# serializers.py

from rest_framework import serializers
from .models import BlogPost

class BlogPostSerializer(serializers.ModelSerializer):
    class Meta:
        model = BlogPost
```

```
        fields = ['id', 'title', 'content',
'author', 'created_at', 'updated_at']
```

In this example:

- `BlogPostSerializer` inherits from `serializers.ModelSerializer`.
- The `Meta` class specifies the model (`BlogPost`) and the fields that should be included in the serialized data.

Step 3: Create Views for the API

DRF offers a variety of ways to handle API views. One of the most efficient ways is to use **ViewSets**, which automatically provide actions like `list`, `create`, `retrieve`, `update`, and `destroy`.

Here's how you can create a `BlogPostViewSet` to handle CRUD operations for the `BlogPost` model:

python

```python
# views.py

from rest_framework import viewsets
from .models import BlogPost
from .serializers import BlogPostSerializer

class BlogPostViewSet(viewsets.ModelViewSet):
    queryset = BlogPost.objects.all()
```

```
serializer_class = BlogPostSerializer
```

In this example:

- `BlogPostViewSet` inherits from `viewsets.ModelViewSet`, which automatically provides behavior for CRUD operations.
- The `queryset` defines which objects are returned by the API (in this case, all blog posts).
- The `serializer_class` tells DRF which serializer to use to convert the model data to JSON.

Step 4: Set Up URLs for the API

Now, let's set up URLs to access the blog post API. DRF uses **routers** to automatically generate URL patterns for viewsets.

First, create a `urls.py` file in your app directory (if it doesn't already exist):

python

```python
# urls.py

from django.urls import path, include
from rest_framework.routers import DefaultRouter
from .views import BlogPostViewSet

router = DefaultRouter()
```

```
router.register(r'posts', BlogPostViewSet)

urlpatterns = [
    path('api/', include(router.urls)),
]
```

In this example:

- We create a `DefaultRouter` instance, which automatically generates the URLs for the viewset actions.
- We register the `BlogPostViewSet` with the router, so the API endpoints will be automatically created for actions like `list`, `create`, `retrieve`, `update`, and `destroy`.
- The `api/` prefix in the `urlpatterns` ensures that the API URLs are accessible under `/api/posts/`.

Step 5: Testing the API

Once you've set up the viewset and URLs, you can now test your API. To run the development server, use the following command:

```bash
bash
```

```
python manage.py runserver
```

You can then visit the following URLs in your browser or use tools like **Postman** or **curl** to interact with your API:

- **GET /api/posts/**: Retrieve all blog posts.
- **POST /api/posts/**: Create a new blog post.
- **GET /api/posts/{id}/**: Retrieve a single blog post by ID.
- **PUT /api/posts/{id}/**: Update a blog post by ID.
- **DELETE /api/posts/{id}/**: Delete a blog post by ID.

You can also visit the **Browsable API** provided by DRF at `http://127.0.0.1:8000/api/posts/`, where you can interact with the API directly from your browser.

Real-World Example: Building an API for Your Blog App

Let's create a complete example of a simple API for managing blog posts in a blog app. We'll cover setting up serializers, views, and URLs, and show how to interact with the API to retrieve and create blog posts.

Step 1: Define the BlogPost Model

Let's start by defining the `BlogPost` model (we've already defined this in previous chapters):

```python
# models.py

from django.db import models
```

```python
class BlogPost(models.Model):
    title = models.CharField(max_length=200)
    content = models.TextField()
    author = models.CharField(max_length=100)
    created_at                          =
models.DateTimeField(auto_now_add=True)
    updated_at                          =
models.DateTimeField(auto_now=True)

    def __str__(self):
        return self.title
```

Step 2: Create the Serializer

We'll create a serializer to convert `BlogPost` model instances to JSON:

python

```python
# serializers.py

from rest_framework import serializers
from .models import BlogPost

class
BlogPostSerializer(serializers.ModelSerializer)
:
    class Meta:
        model = BlogPost
```

```
        fields = ['id', 'title', 'content',
'author', 'created_at', 'updated_at']
```

Step 3: Create the ViewSet

Now, create the `BlogPostViewSet` to handle the CRUD operations for blog posts:

python

```
# views.py

from rest_framework import viewsets
from .models import BlogPost
from .serializers import BlogPostSerializer

class BlogPostViewSet(viewsets.ModelViewSet):
    queryset = BlogPost.objects.all()
    serializer_class = BlogPostSerializer
```

Step 4: Set Up the URLs

Set up the router to automatically generate the API URLs for the `BlogPostViewSet`:

python

```
# urls.py

from django.urls import path, include
from rest_framework.routers import DefaultRouter
```

```
from .views import BlogPostViewSet

router = DefaultRouter()
router.register(r'posts', BlogPostViewSet)

urlpatterns = [
    path('api/', include(router.urls)),
]
```

Step 5: Testing the API

To test the API, run the development server:

```bash
bash
```

```
python manage.py runserver
```

Visit `http://127.0.0.1:8000/api/posts/` in your browser to access the **Browsable API**. You can interact with the API to create, update, delete, and view blog posts.

For example, you can:

- **Create a new blog post** by sending a POST request with JSON data like this:

```json
json
```

```
{
    "title": "My First Blog Post",
```

```
    "content": "This is the content of my first
blog post.",
    "author": "John Doe"
}
```

- **View blog posts** by sending a `GET` request to `/api/posts/`.
- **Update a blog post** by sending a `PUT` request with new data to `/api/posts/{id}/`.
- **Delete a blog post** by sending a `DELETE` request to `/api/posts/{id}/`.

Summary

In this chapter, we introduced **Django Rest Framework (DRF)** and explored how to build a RESTful API for your Django application. We covered the following topics:

- **Installing DRF** and setting it up with Django.
- **Serializers**: Converting Django models into JSON format.
- **Viewsets**: Automatically handling CRUD operations with Django's `ModelViewSet`.
- **URLs**: Using DRF's routers to automatically generate API endpoints.

157

- **Real-world example**: Building an API to manage blog posts, including retrieving, creating, updating, and deleting posts.

With DRF, creating a powerful and flexible API is quick and easy. In the next chapter, we'll dive into **authentication and permissions** in DRF, enabling you to secure your API and control access based on user roles.

CHAPTER 14

DJANGO MIDDLEWARE: CUSTOMIZING REQUEST AND RESPONSE FLOW

Understanding Django Middleware

In Django, **middleware** is a framework of hooks that allows you to process requests globally before they reach the view and process responses before they are returned to the client. Middleware can be used for a variety of purposes, including handling authentication, logging, session management, and modifying the request or response objects.

Django middleware operates on the request/response cycle, which can be broken down as follows:

1. **Request phase**: A request is received by Django. Middleware can modify the request before it reaches the view.

2. **View phase**: The request is passed to the view function, where the main processing occurs.

3. **Response phase**: The view generates a response, which can be modified by middleware before it is sent back to the client.

Middleware is executed in the order it is defined in the MIDDLEWARE setting in settings.py. It can operate on both the request and the response, enabling various kinds of global processing.

Creating Custom Middleware for Additional Functionality

Creating custom middleware in Django is straightforward. You need to create a class that implements at least one of the following methods:

- **__init__**: This method is called when the middleware is initialized.
- **__call__**: This method processes the request or response.
- **process_request**: This method processes the request before it reaches the view.
- **process_response**: This method processes the response before it is sent back to the client.

A custom middleware class in Django should inherit from MiddlewareMixin or, in Django 1.10 and later, it can simply inherit from object if it only implements __call__.

Here's a basic structure of a custom middleware class:

python

160

```python
from        django.utils.deprecation        import
MiddlewareMixin

class CustomMiddleware(MiddlewareMixin):
    def process_request(self, request):
        # Code to process the incoming request
        print("Processing            request:",
request.path)

    def     process_response(self,     request,
response):
        # Code to modify the outgoing response
        response['X-Processed-By']            =
'CustomMiddleware'
        print("Processing            response:",
response.status_code)
        return response
```

In this example:

- `process_request`: This method is called on every incoming request. You can use this to check things like authentication or log the request.
- `process_response`: This method is called after the view has processed the request, allowing you to modify the response before it's sent back to the client.

To enable this middleware, add it to the MIDDLEWARE setting in `settings.py`:

```
python

# settings.py

MIDDLEWARE = [
    # other middleware
    'myapp.middleware.CustomMiddleware',   # Add
the custom middleware
]
```

Django will process this middleware in the order it's listed, so be sure to place it in the right position depending on when you want it to execute (e.g., before or after certain built-in middleware).

Real-World Example: Implementing a Logging Middleware

One of the most common uses for custom middleware is logging. Middleware allows you to log information about incoming requests and outgoing responses, which can be very useful for debugging, auditing, or monitoring traffic.

Let's build a **logging middleware** that logs details about each request and response, including the URL path, request method, and the status code of the response.

Step 1: Creating the Logging Middleware

Create a file called `middleware.py` inside your Django app (if you don't have one) and define the logging middleware:

```python

# middleware.py

import logging

# Set up a logger
logger = logging.getLogger(__name__)

class LoggingMiddleware:
    def __init__(self, get_response):
        # This is called once when the middleware
is initialized
        self.get_response = get_response


    def __call__(self, request):
        # This is called for every incoming
request
        logger.info(f"Request: {request.method}
{request.path}")

        # Process the request
        response = self.get_response(request)

        # This is called for every outgoing
response
        logger.info(f"Response:
{response.status_code} {request.path}")
```

```
return response
```

In this example:

- **__init__**: The `get_response` argument is a callable that will process the request and return a response. We save it to be called later.
- **__call__**: This method processes the incoming request and outgoing response. We use Python's built-in `logging` module to log the HTTP method (GET, POST, etc.), URL path, and the response status code.

Step 2: Configure Logging

In your `settings.py`, add the logging configuration to specify where to save the log messages (e.g., in a file or the console). Here's an example configuration that logs to the console:

python

```python
# settings.py

LOGGING = {
    'version': 1,
    'disable_existing_loggers': False,
    'handlers': {
        'console': {
            'level': 'INFO',
            'class': 'logging.StreamHandler',
```

```
            },
        },
        'loggers': {
            'django': {
                'handlers': ['console'],
                'level': 'INFO',
                'propagate': True,
            },
        },
}
```

This configuration logs messages at the INFO level to the console. You can change the handler to log to a file, database, or external service as needed.

Step 3: Add the Middleware to Django Settings

Now that the logging middleware is defined, add it to your MIDDLEWARE setting in settings.py:

python

```
# settings.py

MIDDLEWARE = [
    # other middleware
    'myapp.middleware.LoggingMiddleware',  # Add
the logging middleware
]
```

This will activate the logging middleware. Each time a request is processed, Django will log the HTTP method and URL path, along with the status code of the response.

Step 4: Testing the Logging Middleware

To test the logging middleware, run the development server:

bash

```
python manage.py runserver
```

Now, when you make requests to your Django application, you should see log messages in the console like this:

ruby

```
INFO:__main__:Request: GET /home/
INFO:__main__:Response: 200 /home/
```

The log messages will provide useful information about the HTTP requests and responses, helping you monitor and debug your application.

Additional Middleware Features

Django's middleware framework is powerful and flexible, and it allows you to do much more than just logging. Here are some additional things you can do with custom middleware:

- **Authentication and Authorization**: You can check if a user is authenticated before passing the request to the view, or you can implement custom permission checks.

  Example:

  ```python
  python
  ```

  ```python
  #   Middleware   for   checking   user
  authentication
  if not request.user.is_authenticated:
      return redirect('login')
  ```

- **Modifying the Request**: You can modify the request object before it reaches the view. For example, you could add custom headers or data to the request.

  Example:

  ```python
  python
  ```

  ```python
  # Adding a custom header to the request
  ```

167

```
request.META['HTTP_X_CUSTOM_HEADER']     =
'Custom Value'
```

- **Modifying the Response**: You can modify the response before it is sent back to the client. For example, you can add custom headers, compress the response, or modify the content.

  Example:

  ```python
  python
  ```

  ```
  # Adding a custom header to the response
  response['X-Custom-Header']    =    'Header
  Value'
  ```

- **Exception Handling**: You can use middleware to catch exceptions and handle them globally, such as logging them or displaying a custom error page.

Summary

In this chapter, we learned about **Django middleware** and how it allows you to customize the request/response flow. We covered:

- **The role of middleware** in Django, including how it processes requests and responses.

- **Creating custom middleware** by implementing the `process_request` and `process_response` methods or using the `__call__` method.

- **Real-world example**: Implementing a **logging middleware** that logs incoming requests and outgoing responses, which is useful for debugging and monitoring.

- **Additional middleware functionality**: We discussed how to modify the request and response, handle authentication, and manage exceptions.

Middleware is a powerful tool for customizing the behavior of your Django application. In the next chapter, we'll explore **testing** in Django, where we'll learn how to write tests for your views, models, and middleware to ensure your application works as expected.

CHAPTER 15

CACHING IN DJANGO: SPEEDING UP YOUR WEB APP

Introduction to Caching in Django

Caching is a technique used to store frequently accessed data in a temporary storage location so that future requests can retrieve it faster. This is particularly useful for web applications that need to process the same data repeatedly, as caching helps reduce the load on databases and improves response times.

Django offers a flexible caching framework that can cache various components of your application, such as database queries, views, templates, and even static files. By caching the results of expensive operations or frequently requested data, you can greatly improve the performance of your web app.

Django supports several caching strategies, including **in-memory caching**, **file-based caching**, and **database caching**, and it provides a simple API for implementing these strategies.

In this chapter, we'll cover the basics of Django's caching framework, explore the different types of caching available, and provide a real-world example of implementing caching to speed up blog post views.

Types of Caching: Memory, Database, and File Caching

1. Memory Caching (In-Memory Caching)

In-memory caching stores data in the server's memory (RAM). This is the fastest type of caching because it avoids disk I/O. However, in-memory caches are volatile, meaning that the data is lost when the server restarts.

Django provides **Memcached** and **Redis** as popular in-memory caching backends, but for simple use cases, Django also has a default **local-memory cache**.

How to Use In-Memory Caching

You can configure the in-memory cache by setting up CACHES in your settings.py file:

python

```
# settings.py

CACHES = {
    'default': {
        'BACKEND':
'django.core.cache.backends.locmem.LocMemCache'
,   # In-memory cache
        'LOCATION':   'unique-snowflake',      #
Unique identifier for your cache
    }
```

```
}
```

In this example, Django will store the cached data in memory, making it fast but non-persistent.

2. Database Caching

Database caching stores data in your database. It is slower than memory caching but can be useful for caching data that must persist across server restarts. Django uses a database table to store cached data.

To use database caching, configure the CACHES setting with the `django.core.cache.backends.db.DatabaseCache` backend:

python

```python
# settings.py

CACHES = {
    'default': {
        'BACKEND':
'django.core.cache.backends.db.DatabaseCache',
        'LOCATION': 'django_cache_table',  # The
name of the cache table in your database
    }
}
```

You also need to create the cache table by running the following command:

```bash
python manage.py createcachetable
```

Database caching is ideal when you need to persist cached data across server restarts, but it is slower compared to in-memory caching.

3. File Caching

File caching stores cached data on disk in files. It is slower than memory caching but can be more scalable because it doesn't rely on memory, and it is more persistent than in-memory caching.

To use file caching, configure CACHES with the django.core.cache.backends.filebased.FileBasedCache backend:

```python
# settings.py

CACHES = {
    'default': {
```

```
    'BACKEND':
'django.core.cache.backends.filebased.FileBased
Cache',
    'LOCATION':  '/path/to/cache/directory',
# The directory where cached files will be stored
    }
}
```

File caching is useful when you need to persist cached data across server restarts and don't mind the extra overhead of disk I/O. It is slower than memory caching but can be more scalable.

Real-World Example: Implementing Caching for Blog Post Views

Now that we understand the different types of caching, let's implement caching for blog post views in a real-world example. This will improve the performance of your blog app by caching the response of the blog post detail page, which is frequently requested and potentially expensive to generate (especially if the blog post content is dynamic or involves database queries).

Step 1: Enable Caching in Django Settings

For this example, let's use **file-based caching** to store the cached content of the blog post pages. In your settings.py, configure the caching backend:

```python
python
```

174

```
# settings.py

CACHES = {
    'default': {
        'BACKEND':
'django.core.cache.backends.filebased.FileBased
Cache',
        'LOCATION': '/path/to/cache/directory',
    }
}
```

Make sure to replace /path/to/cache/directory with the actual path where you want to store cached files. The cache directory should be writable by the server.

Step 2: Apply Caching to the Blog Post View

Next, we'll add caching to the blog post detail view. Django provides a cache_page decorator that allows you to cache the entire view for a specified amount of time. For example, we can cache the blog post detail page for 15 minutes:

python

```
# views.py

from    django.shortcuts    import    render,
get_object_or_404
```

```
from    django.views.decorators.cache    import
cache_page
from .models import BlogPost

@cache_page(60 * 15)   # Cache this view for 15
minutes (900 seconds)
def blog_detail(request, pk):
    post = get_object_or_404(BlogPost, pk=pk)
    return                         render(request,
'blog/blog_detail.html', {'post': post})
```

In this example:

- The cache_page(60 * 15) decorator caches the entire blog post view for 15 minutes.
- This means that if the same user (or another user) accesses the same blog post within the next 15 minutes, Django will serve the cached version of the page, avoiding the need to fetch data from the database or render the page again.

Step 3: Clearing the Cache

One potential issue with caching is that if you update the content (e.g., editing a blog post), the cached version might not reflect the changes immediately. To handle this, you can manually clear the cache whenever a blog post is updated or deleted.

Here's an example of how you can clear the cache for a specific blog post when it is updated:

python

```python
# views.py

from django.core.cache import cache
from django.shortcuts import render, get_object_or_404
from .models import BlogPost

def blog_update(request, pk):
    post = get_object_or_404(BlogPost, pk=pk)
    # Update the blog post (form handling and saving logic here)
    post.save()

    # Clear the cached blog post detail view
    cache.delete(f'blog_post_{pk}')

    return render(request, 'blog/blog_detail.html', {'post': post})
```

In this example:

- After updating the blog post, we clear the cache for the specific blog post detail view using `cache.delete(f'blog_post_{pk}')`. The key used to delete the cache should match the one Django uses for caching the view (we can use the `pk` to generate a unique cache key).

Step 4: Testing Caching

Now, run the development server and access a blog post detail page. After the first request, you should notice a faster response time, since the content is served from the cache.

You can verify that the cache is working by making a change to the blog post and observing that the cached version is cleared and updated. Django will automatically serve the updated version of the page after the cache is cleared.

Summary

In this chapter, we explored **caching** in Django and how it can improve the performance of your web application by reducing database queries and speeding up response times. We covered:

- **Types of caching** in Django: memory caching, database caching, and file caching.
- **Configuring caching** in Django by setting up the CACHES setting in `settings.py`.

- **Using the `cache_page` decorator** to cache views and improve the speed of frequently accessed pages.
- **Clearing the cache** when content is updated to ensure that changes are reflected immediately.

By implementing caching for the blog post views, we significantly improved the performance of our blog app. In the next chapter, we will explore **database optimization techniques** in Django to further enhance the performance and scalability of your application.

CHAPTER 16

MANAGING SESSIONS AND COOKIES

Understanding Sessions and Cookies in Django

In web applications, **sessions** and **cookies** are essential mechanisms for storing information between requests. They allow you to remember user-specific data (like logged-in status or preferences) across different pages and visits.

- **Cookies** are small pieces of data sent by the server to the client (usually the web browser) and stored locally. They are often used to store data like user preferences, authentication tokens, or session IDs. Cookies are sent back to the server with every request to the domain that set them.

- **Sessions** are a higher-level concept built on top of cookies. In Django, sessions are used to store user-specific data on the server side. A session is typically identified by a unique session ID stored in a cookie on the client-side. The actual session data is stored on the server, either in the database, file system, or cache, which provides a more secure way to store user information than cookies alone.

180

Django provides a built-in **session framework** that makes it easy to store and retrieve session data.

Storing User Data with Sessions

Step 1: Enabling Sessions in Django

By default, Django's session framework is enabled. Django stores session data using a session ID that is sent to the user's browser as a cookie (usually called `sessionid`). This cookie is used to identify the session on subsequent requests. Django automatically creates and manages this session ID cookie for you.

The session data is stored on the server side, and the backend for storing sessions can be configured to use different storage options (e.g., the database, file system, or cache).

The session settings in `settings.py` look like this by default:

```python
```

```python
# settings.py

# Session settings
SESSION_ENGINE                                   =
'django.contrib.sessions.backends.db'    #  Using
the database to store sessions
```

```
SESSION_COOKIE_NAME = 'sessionid'  # The name of
the session cookie
```

In this configuration:

- **SESSION_ENGINE**: Specifies the session backend. Django provides several backends, including database-backed sessions (`django.contrib.sessions.backends.db`), file-based sessions (`django.contrib.sessions.backends.file`), and cache-based sessions (`django.contrib.sessions.backends.cache`).
- **SESSION_COOKIE_NAME**: Specifies the name of the session cookie.

Step 2: Using Sessions to Store Data

To use sessions in Django, you can access the `request.session` dictionary, which behaves like a normal Python dictionary. You can store, modify, and retrieve data from the session.

Here's an example of using sessions to store user data:

```
python
```

```
# views.py
```

```
from django.shortcuts import render

def set_user_preference(request):
    # Store data in the session
    request.session['preferred_language']    =
'English'
    return                     render(request,
'preference_set.html')

def get_user_preference(request):
    # Retrieve data from the session
    preferred_language                       =
request.session.get('preferred_language',   'Not
set')
    return                     render(request,
'show_preference.html',   {'preferred_language':
preferred_language})
```

In this example:

- `request.session['preferred_language']` stores
  the user's preferred language.
- `request.session.get('preferred_language',`
  `'Not set')` retrieves the stored language preference, or
  returns `'Not set'` if the preference is not available.

Django automatically saves session data between requests, so you
don't need to worry about manually saving or loading session data.

Step 3: Expiring Sessions

Sessions can be set to expire after a certain period of inactivity. In Django, you can configure session expiration using the SESSION_COOKIE_AGE setting:

python

```
# settings.py

# Session cookie will expire after 3600 seconds
(1 hour)
SESSION_COOKIE_AGE = 3600
```

You can also set SESSION_EXPIRE_AT_BROWSER_CLOSE to True to expire the session when the user closes the browser:

python

```
# settings.py

SESSION_EXPIRE_AT_BROWSER_CLOSE = True
```

Cookies in Django

While sessions store data server-side, **cookies** store data client-side. In Django, you can manage cookies using request and response objects.

184

Step 1: Setting Cookies

To set a cookie in Django, you use the
`HttpResponse.set_cookie()` method:

python

```
# views.py

from django.http import HttpResponse

def set_cookie(request):
    response = HttpResponse("Cookie Set!")
    response.set_cookie('user_language',
'English')
    return response
```

In this example, the `set_cookie` method sets a cookie called
`user_language` with the value `English`. This cookie will be
sent to the client's browser and will be included in future requests
to the server.

Step 2: Getting Cookies

To retrieve a cookie, you use `request.COOKIES`:

python

```
# views.py
```

```
from django.http import HttpResponse

def get_cookie(request):
    user_language                          =
request.COOKIES.get('user_language', 'Not Set')
    return      HttpResponse(f'User      Language:
{user_language}')
```

In this example, `request.COOKIES.get('user_language',
'Not Set')` retrieves the `user_language` cookie. If the cookie
is not set, it returns the default value `'Not Set'`.

Step 3: Deleting Cookies

To delete a cookie, you use the
`HttpResponse.delete_cookie()` method:

python

```
# views.py

from django.http import HttpResponse

def delete_cookie(request):
    response = HttpResponse("Cookie Deleted!")
    response.delete_cookie('user_language')
    return response
```

This deletes the `user_language` cookie by calling `delete_cookie`.

Real-World Example: Implementing a Cart System for an E-Commerce Site

Now, let's use **sessions** and **cookies** to implement a simple shopping cart system for an e-commerce site. In this system:

- The cart will be stored in the session, so it will persist between pages.
- The cart items will be stored in a cookie so that the cart can persist even if the user logs out or closes the browser.

Step 1: Define the Cart View

Let's define views to add items to the cart, view the cart, and remove items from the cart. For simplicity, we will use the product's ID and quantity in the cart.

python

```python
# views.py

from django.shortcuts import render, redirect
from django.http import HttpResponse
from .models import Product
```

```python
def add_to_cart(request, product_id):
    # Get the product from the database
    product = Product.objects.get(id=product_id)

    # Get the cart from the session, or create an
empty cart if it doesn't exist
    cart = request.session.get('cart', {})

    # Add the product to the cart
    cart[product_id] = cart.get(product_id, 0) +
1  # Increment quantity by 1
    request.session['cart'] = cart  # Save the
updated cart in the session

    return redirect('view_cart')

def view_cart(request):
    cart = request.session.get('cart', {})

    # Retrieve product details for the items in
the cart
    products = []
    total_price = 0
    for product_id, quantity in cart.items():
        product                              =
Product.objects.get(id=product_id)
        total_price += product.price * quantity
```

```
        products.append({'product':       product,
'quantity': quantity})


    return    render(request,    'view_cart.html',
{'products':         products,        'total_price':
total_price})


def remove_from_cart(request, product_id):
    cart = request.session.get('cart', {})


    # Remove  the  product  from  the  cart  if  it
exists
    if product_id in cart:
        del cart[product_id]


    request.session['cart'] = cart   # Save  the
updated cart in the session
    return redirect('view_cart')
```

In these views:

- `add_to_cart`: Adds a product to the cart stored in the session. If the product is already in the cart, it increments the quantity by 1.
- `view_cart`: Displays the items in the cart along with the total price.
- `remove_from_cart`: Removes a product from the cart.

Step 2: Create the Cart Template

In `view_cart.html`, we will display the products in the cart and allow users to remove items:

html

```
<!-- view_cart.html -->

<h1>Your Shopping Cart</h1>
<ul>
    {% for item in products %}
        <li>
            {{ item.product.name }} - Quantity:
{{    item.quantity    }}    -    Price:    ${{
item.product.price }}
            <a href="{% url 'remove_from_cart'
item.product.id %}">Remove</a>
        </li>
    {% empty %}
        <p>Your cart is empty.</p>
    {% endfor %}
</ul>

<p>Total Price: ${{ total_price }}</p>
```

Step 3: Define URLs

In `urls.py`, define the URL patterns for adding, viewing, and removing items from the cart:

```python

# urls.py

from django.urls import path
from . import views

urlpatterns = [
    path('add_to_cart/<int:product_id>/',
views.add_to_cart, name='add_to_cart'),
    path('view_cart/',          views.view_cart,
name='view_cart'),
    path('remove_from_cart/<int:product_id>/',
views.remove_from_cart,
name='remove_from_cart'),
]
```

Summary

In this chapter, we explored how to manage **sessions** and **cookies** in Django:

- **Sessions** are stored server-side and can be used to store user-specific data across requests. We used sessions to implement a shopping cart system that persists across different pages.
- **Cookies** are stored client-side and can be used to remember user preferences or store authentication tokens.

We discussed setting, getting, and deleting cookies in Django.

- We implemented a **cart system** for an e-commerce site, using sessions to store the cart and allowing users to add, view, and remove items from the cart.

By using Django's built-in session and cookie handling, we can easily store and manage user data, making it persistent across requests and user sessions. In the next chapter, we will explore **file uploads** in Django and how to handle user-uploaded files securely and efficiently.

CHAPTER 17

TESTING DJANGO WEB APPS

Introduction to Unit Testing and Test-Driven Development (TDD)

Unit testing is a software testing technique where individual units or components of a program are tested in isolation to ensure they work as expected. In the context of Django, unit tests typically focus on testing views, models, forms, and other components of your application. The goal of unit testing is to catch bugs early, ensure code correctness, and make future changes easier by providing a safety net of tests.

Test-Driven Development (TDD) is a software development methodology where you write tests before writing the actual code. TDD follows a simple cycle:

1. **Write a test**: Write a test for a small unit of functionality that your application should have.
2. **Run the test**: At this point, the test will fail because the functionality isn't implemented yet.
3. **Write the code**: Write the minimal amount of code necessary to pass the test.
4. **Refactor**: Refactor the code to improve its structure, then rerun the tests to make sure everything still works.

TDD encourages you to think about your application's behavior before implementation and ensures that your code is always covered by tests, which reduces bugs and increases confidence in your code.

Django provides an extensive testing framework that integrates with Python's built-in **unittest** module. Django's testing tools allow you to write automated tests for your models, views, templates, and forms.

Using Django's Testing Tools and Framework

Django's TestCase Class

Django's testing framework is built on top of Python's `unittest` module and provides a custom `TestCase` class that includes helper methods for testing Django applications.

The `TestCase` class provides methods to:

- Set up and tear down test data.
- Make requests to views and assert the response status.
- Check if models are saved correctly in the database.
- Ensure templates render as expected.

Each test is written as a method of a class that inherits from `django.test.TestCase`. By default, Django tests use a separate test database, which is created and destroyed

194

automatically for each test run, ensuring that tests do not affect production data.

Step 1: Setting Up the Test Class

Here's how you can create a simple test class in Django. This test class checks if a model is saving correctly and if a view returns the correct response.

python

```python
# tests.py

from django.test import TestCase
from django.urls import reverse
from .models import BlogPost

class BlogPostModelTest(TestCase):
    def setUp(self):
        # This method is called before each test
        self.post = BlogPost.objects.create(
            title="Test Post",
            content="This is a test blog post.",
            author="Test Author"
        )

    def test_blog_post_creation(self):
        # Test that the blog post was created
successfully
```

```
        post = BlogPost.objects.get(title="Test
Post")
        self.assertEqual(post.author,      "Test
Author")
        self.assertEqual(post.content, "This is
a test blog post.")

class BlogPostViewTest(TestCase):
    def test_blog_post_list_view(self):
        # Test the blog post list view
        response                           =
self.client.get(reverse('blog_list'))
        self.assertEqual(response.status_code,
200)
        self.assertTemplateUsed(response,
'blog/blog_list.html')
        self.assertContains(response,      "Test
Post")
```

In this example:

- **setUp**: This method is called before each test method to set up the test environment. We use it to create a BlogPost instance for our tests.
- **test_blog_post_creation**: This test verifies that the blog post is created correctly in the database and that its fields match the expected values.
- **test_blog_post_list_view**: This test makes an HTTP GET request to the blog_list view and checks

that the response is successful (status code 200), the correct template is used, and the content is included in the response.

Step 2: Running Tests

To run your tests, use the following Django management command:

bash

```
python manage.py test
```

Django will automatically discover tests in any file named `tests.py` inside your application directories. It will create a test database, run all the tests, and provide a summary of the results.

If your tests pass, you'll see an output like this:

markdown

```
..........................................
..........................................
......
--------------------------------------------------
---------------------
Ran 100 tests in 2.341s

OK
```

If any tests fail, Django will show detailed error messages so you can debug the problem.

Real-World Example: Writing Tests for Blog Views and Models

In this section, we will write tests for both the **views** and **models** of a simple blog app. We will create tests to:

1. Check if a blog post is created and stored correctly.
2. Test if the blog post list view displays the correct content.
3. Test if the blog post detail view works properly.

Step 1: Writing Tests for Blog Models

Let's start by writing a test for the BlogPost model. We want to ensure that a blog post can be created and saved correctly.

python

```python
# tests.py

from django.test import TestCase
from .models import BlogPost

class BlogPostModelTest(TestCase):
    def setUp(self):
        self.post = BlogPost.objects.create(
            title="Test Blog Post",
```

```
            content="This   is   a   test   blog   post
content.",
            author="Test Author"
        )


    def test_blog_post_creation(self):
        post = BlogPost.objects.get(title="Test
Blog Post")
        self.assertEqual(post.title, "Test Blog
Post")
        self.assertEqual(post.content, "This is
a test blog post content.")
        self.assertEqual(post.author,       "Test
Author")
        self.assertIsNotNone(post.created_at)   #
Check if the creation timestamp is set
```

In this test:

- We use `setUp` to create a blog post instance before running the test.
- The `test_blog_post_creation` method checks if the blog post is saved correctly, verifying that the title, content, and author are correct and ensuring the `created_at` timestamp is set.

199

Step 2: Writing Tests for Blog Views

Now let's write tests for the views in our blog app. We'll test the
`blog_list` view to ensure that it renders the correct template and
contains the expected content.

python

```python
# tests.py

from django.test import TestCase
from django.urls import reverse
from .models import BlogPost

class BlogPostViewTest(TestCase):
    def setUp(self):
        self.post = BlogPost.objects.create(
            title="Test Blog Post",
            content="This is a test blog post
content.",
            author="Test Author"
        )

    def test_blog_post_list_view(self):
        # Test the blog post list view
        response                                  =
self.client.get(reverse('blog_list'))
        self.assertEqual(response.status_code,
200)  # Check if the status code is 200
```

```
        self.assertTemplateUsed(response,
'blog/blog_list.html')   # Ensure the correct
template is used
        self.assertContains(response, "Test Blog
Post")  # Check if the post title appears in the
response

    def test_blog_post_detail_view(self):
        # Test the blog post detail view
        response                               =
self.client.get(reverse('blog_detail',
args=[self.post.id]))
        self.assertEqual(response.status_code,
200)  # Ensure status code is 200
        self.assertTemplateUsed(response,
'blog/blog_detail.html')    # Ensure correct
template is used
        self.assertContains(response, "Test Blog
Post")  # Ensure post content is displayed in the
response
```

In these tests:

- **test_blog_post_list_view**: This test ensures that the blog list view returns a 200 status code, uses the correct template, and includes the title of the test blog post.

- **test_blog_post_detail_view**: This test checks that the blog post detail view works correctly by verifying the

201

status code, the template used, and the presence of the blog post's title.

Step 3: Running the Tests

After writing the tests, run the following command to execute the tests:

bash

```
python manage.py test
```

If all tests pass, you should see output indicating that everything is working as expected.

Summary

In this chapter, we learned about **unit testing** and **Test-Driven Development (TDD)** in Django. We covered:

- **Unit testing**: Writing tests for individual components of your application to ensure they behave correctly.
- **Test-Driven Development (TDD)**: A methodology where tests are written before code to help guide development and ensure that all functionality is covered by tests.

- **Django's testing framework**: Using Django's `TestCase` class to write tests for views, models, and other components, along with helper methods like `setUp()`, `assertEqual()`, and `assertContains()`.
- **Real-world example**: Writing tests for the blog app's models and views, including checking that blog posts are created and displayed correctly.

By following TDD principles and writing tests for your application, you can ensure that your code is robust, reliable, and easier to maintain in the future. In the next chapter, we will explore **deployment** strategies for Django applications, including how to deploy your app to production using services like Heroku and AWS.

CHAPTER 18

DEBUGGING AND TROUBLESHOOTING DJANGO APPLICATIONS

Common Django Errors and How to Troubleshoot Them

As with any web application, Django developers encounter errors and issues during development. Understanding the common errors and knowing how to troubleshoot them effectively is a vital skill. In this chapter, we will explore some common Django errors, how to identify them, and how to fix them.

1. 500 Internal Server Error

A **500 Internal Server Error** indicates that something went wrong on the server side, but the specific error isn't exposed to the user. This is a common error during development and can be caused by a variety of issues, such as misconfigurations, syntax errors, or issues in the view or model logic.

How to troubleshoot:

- Check the server logs for detailed error messages. Django's debug mode (enabled in `settings.py` with `DEBUG = True`) will show detailed error messages.
- Look at the traceback to pinpoint where the error occurred. You can view the error messages in the terminal or in the Django development server's output.

2. 404 Not Found

A **404 Not Found** error occurs when a URL is requested that doesn't exist in the application. This can happen if there is a typo in the URL, the route is not correctly configured, or the URL is missing from the `urls.py` file.

How to troubleshoot:

- Ensure that the URL pattern exists in your `urls.py` file and is properly mapped to the corresponding view.
- Check for typos in the URL or the view function name.
- Make sure that the correct HTTP methods (GET, POST, etc.) are used for the view.

3. Form Validation Errors

Form validation errors are one of the most common issues in Django applications. These errors occur when the form data is not valid according to the form fields or custom validation rules.

How to troubleshoot:

- Check the form's `is_valid()` method to determine if the form is passing validation.
- Inspect the error messages in the form using `form.errors` to understand why the form is not valid. Django provides useful error messages for each field that failed validation.
- Ensure that required fields are being passed in the form, and check for missing or incorrect input types.

4. Database Errors

Database-related errors often occur when there is an issue with database migrations, queries, or the database connection itself.

How to troubleshoot:

- Check the database settings in `settings.py` to ensure the correct database engine and credentials are configured.
- Run `python manage.py makemigrations` and `python manage.py migrate` to ensure that the database schema is up to date with the models.
- Look at the traceback to see if the error is caused by a query, and ensure that the database table and field names are correct.

5. Template Errors

Template errors occur when Django encounters issues while rendering a template. Common errors include missing context variables, invalid template tags, or syntax errors in templates.

How to troubleshoot:

- Check the error message to determine which template variable is causing the issue. Django will usually provide details such as "Variable x does not exist."
- Ensure that all required context variables are passed to the template from the view.
- Review the template syntax to ensure it is correct, especially with tags like {% for %} and {% if %}.

Using Django's Debugging Tools

Django provides several built-in tools and techniques for debugging and troubleshooting errors in your application. Here are some of the most useful tools:

1. Django Debug Mode

Django's debug mode provides detailed error messages and stack traces when an error occurs. You can enable debug mode by setting DEBUG = True in the settings.py file:

```python
# settings.py

DEBUG = True
```

When DEBUG is enabled, Django will display detailed information about errors, including:

- The traceback of the error
- The template or view where the error occurred
- The request data and context

This is extremely useful during development because it allows you to quickly identify and fix errors.

2. Logging in Django

Django supports logging, which allows you to track and log errors, warnings, and other events in your application. You can configure logging in settings.py to capture log messages and save them to a file or console.

Here's a basic logging configuration that logs errors to a file:

```python
# settings.py
```

```
LOGGING = {
    'version': 1,
    'disable_existing_loggers': False,
    'handlers': {
        'file': {
            'level': 'ERROR',
            'class': 'logging.FileHandler',
            'filename': 'django_errors.log',
        },
    },
    'loggers': {
        'django': {
            'handlers': ['file'],
            'level': 'ERROR',
            'propagate': True,
        },
    },
}
```

This will log any errors that occur in your application to a file named django_errors.log.

3. Django Debug Toolbar

The **Django Debug Toolbar** is a third-party tool that provides detailed debugging information for each page request. It shows performance metrics, database queries, request/response headers, and much more in a sidebar that appears on your website during development.

To install it, run:

```bash
pip install django-debug-toolbar
```

Then, add `'debug_toolbar'` to `INSTALLED_APPS` in `settings.py`, and include the middleware:

```python
# settings.py

INSTALLED_APPS = [
    # other apps
    'debug_toolbar',
]

MIDDLEWARE = [
    # other middleware

'debug_toolbar.middleware.DebugToolbarMiddlewar
e',
]

INTERNAL_IPS = ['127.0.0.1']
```

This will allow you to see detailed debugging information on each page of your site.

Real-World Example: Debugging a Broken Form Submission

Let's look at a real-world example where a form submission is not working as expected, and we need to troubleshoot and fix the issue.

Scenario:

We have a contact form that allows users to submit their name, email, and message. However, the form is not being submitted correctly, and the page is not rendering after submission. We need to identify the issue and fix it.

Step 1: Check for Validation Errors

Start by checking if there are any form validation errors. Django automatically validates the form before processing the data, and the `form.errors` attribute contains all the validation messages.

python

```python
# views.py

from django.shortcuts import render
from .forms import ContactForm

def contact_view(request):
    if request.method == 'POST':
```

```
form = ContactForm(request.POST)
if form.is_valid():
    # Process the form data (e.g., send
an email, save to the database)
        return            render(request,
'contact_success.html')
    else:
        # Print form errors to the console
for debugging
        print(form.errors)
        return            render(request,
'contact.html', {'form': form})
else:
    form = ContactForm()
return     render(request,     'contact.html',
{'form': form})
```

In this example:

- We print `form.errors` to the console to see the validation errors in the form.
- If the form is invalid, we return the form with the errors displayed on the page.

Step 2: Inspect the Template

Ensure that the form is being rendered correctly in the template and that the error messages are being displayed. Modify the template to display form errors:

212

```html
html

<!-- contact.html -->

<h1>Contact Us</h1>

<form method="post">
    {% csrf_token %}
    {{ form.as_p }}

    {% if form.errors %}
        <ul>
            {% for field in form %}
                {% for error in field.errors %}
                    <li>{{ error }}</li>
                {% endfor %}
            {% endfor %}
        </ul>
    {% endif %}

    <button type="submit">Submit</button>
</form>
```

In this template:

- We use `{{ form.as_p }}` to render the form fields.
- We display any errors using `form.errors`, which will show a list of validation issues.

Step 3: Check the Form Logic

Check the form logic to ensure that it's correctly handling the data. For example, if you have a custom validation method, verify that it is not causing issues:

python

```python
# forms.py

from django import forms

class ContactForm(forms.Form):
    name = forms.CharField(max_length=100)
    email = forms.EmailField()
    message = forms.CharField(widget=forms.Textarea)

    def clean_message(self):
        message = self.cleaned_data.get('message')
        if len(message) < 10:
            raise forms.ValidationError("Message must be at least 10 characters long.")
        return message
```

In this example:

- The `clean_message` method checks if the message is at least 10 characters long. If the message is too short, it raises a validation error.
- You can print the error messages and inspect the validation process.

Step 4: Debug with Django Debug Toolbar

If the issue is related to database queries or view performance, use the **Django Debug Toolbar** to inspect the database queries, request/response cycle, and other details that can help you identify performance issues.

Once you install and configure the Django Debug Toolbar, it will display useful information directly on the webpage during development, such as:

- SQL queries executed during the page load
- Template rendering time
- Cache hits and misses

Summary

In this chapter, we covered the essential tools and techniques for **debugging and troubleshooting Django applications**:

- Common Django errors, such as 500, 404, and form validation errors, and how to troubleshoot them.
- Django's built-in debugging tools, including **debug mode**, **logging**, and the **Django Debug Toolbar**.
- A real-world example of debugging a broken form submission by checking for validation errors, inspecting templates, and testing the form logic.

By mastering debugging techniques and utilizing Django's built-in tools, you can quickly identify and resolve issues in your web application, ensuring a smoother development experience. In the next chapter, we will cover **deploying Django applications** to production, ensuring your app runs efficiently in a live environment.

CHAPTER 19

SECURITY BEST PRACTICES IN DJANGO

Common Security Threats and How Django Mitigates Them

Web applications are often targeted by attackers seeking to exploit vulnerabilities. Django, being a powerful web framework, includes numerous built-in features to help mitigate common security threats. In this chapter, we will cover some of the most common web security threats and how Django helps protect against them.

1. Cross-Site Scripting (XSS)

Cross-Site Scripting (XSS) attacks occur when an attacker injects malicious JavaScript into a webpage, which is then executed in the context of a user's browser. This can lead to the theft of cookies, session tokens, or other sensitive information.

How Django mitigates XSS:

- **Automatic HTML escaping**: Django automatically escapes variables in templates to prevent JavaScript from being executed in the browser. For example, if a user enters a name that contains a script tag, Django will

217

escape   it   like   this:
```
&lt;script&gt;alert('Hacked!')&lt;/script
&gt;.
```

Example:

```
html
```

```
<p>{{ user_input }}</p>
```

In this case, any malicious JavaScript code entered by the user will be automatically escaped and displayed as plain text, not as executable code.

2. Cross-Site Request Forgery (CSRF)

Cross-Site Request Forgery (CSRF) attacks occur when an attacker tricks a user into submitting a request (such as a form submission) to a web application where they are already authenticated, performing an action the user did not intend.

How Django mitigates CSRF:

- **CSRF tokens**: Django uses a **CSRF token** to ensure that a form submission is made by the user and not by a malicious third-party website. The token is added to the form and checked on the server to verify that the request came from a trusted source.

218

3. SQL Injection

SQL injection occurs when an attacker manipulates SQL queries by injecting malicious SQL code into form fields or URL parameters. This can allow attackers to access or modify sensitive data.

How Django mitigates SQL injection:

- **ORM (Object-Relational Mapping)**: Django's ORM uses parameterized queries, which automatically escape user inputs and prevent SQL injection. Instead of manually constructing raw SQL queries, you use Django's ORM methods to interact with the database safely.

  Example:

  ```python
  # Safe query using Django ORM
  blog_posts                    =
  BlogPost.objects.filter(author='John Doe')
  ```

  In this example, the query is automatically sanitized by Django's ORM, preventing the risk of SQL injection.

4. Session Hijacking and Fixation

Session hijacking occurs when an attacker steals a user's session cookie and uses it to impersonate the user. **Session fixation** occurs when an attacker sets a user's session ID to a known value, allowing them to steal the session later.

How Django mitigates session hijacking and fixation:

- **Secure and HttpOnly cookies**: Django uses the `HttpOnly` and `Secure` flags to protect session cookies. The `HttpOnly` flag prevents JavaScript from accessing the session cookie, and the `Secure` flag ensures the cookie is only sent over HTTPS.
- **Regenerating session IDs**: Django regenerates session IDs after login, making it harder for an attacker to steal and use the session ID.

5. Clickjacking

Clickjacking is a type of attack where an attacker tricks the user into clicking on something different from what the user perceives, potentially causing them to perform actions unknowingly.

How Django mitigates clickjacking:

- **X-Frame-Options**: Django includes the `X-Frame-Options` header to prevent your website from being embedded in an iframe on another site. This header can be set to DENY or SAMEORIGIN to block or restrict framing.

Example:

```python
```

```
# settings.py
X_FRAME_OPTIONS = 'DENY'
```

6. Insecure Deserialization

Insecure deserialization occurs when attackers manipulate serialized objects to execute arbitrary code on the server.

How Django mitigates insecure deserialization:

- Django uses **JSON** or **XML** serialization for transmitting data between the client and server. By avoiding insecure formats like pickle, Django minimizes the risk of insecure deserialization.

Best Practices for Securing Django Applications

Django has many built-in features to help protect your application from security threats. Here are some additional best practices you should follow to further secure your Django web application:

221

1. Use HTTPS (SSL/TLS)

- Ensure that your application is served over HTTPS to encrypt data in transit and protect user privacy.
- In production, configure your web server (e.g., Nginx or Apache) to redirect HTTP traffic to HTTPS.

2. Set the SECURE_SSL_REDIRECT Setting

- If you want to enforce HTTPS across your site, enable the SECURE_SSL_REDIRECT setting to automatically redirect HTTP requests to HTTPS:

```python
# settings.py
SECURE_SSL_REDIRECT = True
```

3. Set Secure and HttpOnly Cookies

- Always set the SESSION_COOKIE_SECURE and CSRF_COOKIE_SECURE settings to ensure that cookies are only sent over HTTPS.

```python
# settings.py
SESSION_COOKIE_SECURE = True
CSRF_COOKIE_SECURE = True
```

4. Regularly Update Django and Dependencies

- Keep your Django version and all dependencies up to date to protect against known vulnerabilities. You can use `pip` to update Django and dependencies:

```bash
bash
```

```bash
pip install --upgrade django
```

5. Limit User Permissions

- Use Django's built-in permissions and groups to restrict user access to sensitive data and actions. Avoid giving users more permissions than they need.

Example:

```python
python
```

```python
# models.py
class BlogPost(models.Model):
    title                      =
models.CharField(max_length=200)
    content = models.TextField()

    class Meta:
        permissions = [
            ("can_edit", "Can edit blog
post"),
```

223

```
]
```

6. Use Strong Passwords

- Django includes a password validation system that ensures users set strong passwords. Enable password validation in `settings.py`:

python

```python
# settings.py
AUTH_PASSWORD_VALIDATORS = [
    {
        'NAME':
'django.contrib.auth.password_validation.
UserAttributeSimilarityValidator',
    },
    {
        'NAME':
'django.contrib.auth.password_validation.
MinimumLengthValidator',
    },
    {
        'NAME':
'django.contrib.auth.password_validation.
CommonPasswordValidator',
    },
    {
```

```
        'NAME':
    'django.contrib.auth.password_validation.
    NumericPasswordValidator',
        },
    ]
```

7. Limit Session Lifespan

- Use Django's session expiration settings to limit how long a session remains active.

```python
# settings.py
SESSION_COOKIE_AGE = 3600   # Set session
timeout to 1 hour
```

8. Disable Debug Mode in Production

- Always set `DEBUG = False` in production to prevent Django from exposing sensitive information, including error details and environment variables.

```python
# settings.py
DEBUG = False
```

225

9. Use Django's secure Middleware

- Enable Django's `SecurityMiddleware` to manage various security features such as SSL redirection, HTTP headers, and session security.

```python
# settings.py
MIDDLEWARE = [

    'django.middleware.security.SecurityMiddleware',
        # other middleware
]
```

Real-World Example: Implementing CSRF Protection for Forms

Cross-Site Request Forgery (CSRF) attacks are a major security concern, but Django provides built-in protection for forms. Here's how you can implement **CSRF protection** for your forms.

Step 1: Enable CSRF Protection

Django's CSRF protection is enabled by default. The key mechanism is the inclusion of a CSRF token in every form. This token is checked with each form submission to verify that the request originated from the legitimate site.

In your form templates, include the `{% csrf_token %}` tag inside the `<form>` tag:

html

```
<!-- contact_form.html -->
<form method="post">
    {% csrf_token %}
    <label for="name">Name:</label>
    <input type="text" name="name" required>
    <label for="message">Message:</label>
    <textarea                       name="message"
required></textarea>
    <button type="submit">Submit</button>
</form>
```

Step 2: Handle CSRF Token Validation in Views

Django will automatically check the CSRF token when processing the form submission. If the token is invalid or missing, Django will return a `403 Forbidden` error.

In your view, ensure the `csrf_protect` decorator is used if you need explicit control:

python

```
# views.py
```

227

```
from     django.views.decorators.csrf     import
csrf_protect
from django.shortcuts import render

@csrf_protect
def contact_view(request):
    if request.method == 'POST':
        # Handle form submission
        pass
    return render(request, 'contact_form.html')
```

Step 3: CSRF Exemptions for APIs (Optional)

For APIs or cases where the CSRF protection is not needed (e.g., APIs using token-based authentication), you can exempt specific views from CSRF protection using the @csrf_exempt decorator:

python

```
# views.py

from     django.views.decorators.csrf     import
csrf_exempt
from django.http import JsonResponse

@csrf_exempt
def api_view(request):
    return   JsonResponse({"message":   "No   CSRF
protection here"})
```

Summary

In this chapter, we explored the importance of **security best practices** in Django and covered:

- **Common security threats** such as XSS, CSRF, SQL injection, and session hijacking, and how Django mitigates them.
- **Best practices** for securing your Django application, including using HTTPS, secure cookies, regular updates, and strong password policies.
- **CSRF protection** for forms, including using Django's `{% csrf_token %}` template tag and the `csrf_protect` decorator.

By following these best practices and utilizing Django's built-in security features, you can build secure and robust Django applications. In the next chapter, we will explore **deploying Django applications** to a production environment, ensuring that your app runs securely and efficiently in a live setting.

CHAPTER 20

DEPLOYING DJANGO APPLICATIONS

Introduction to Deployment Tools (Heroku, DigitalOcean, AWS)

Deploying a Django application is a critical step in moving from development to production. It involves configuring the environment, setting up the necessary servers, ensuring the application is secure, and making it accessible to users. In this chapter, we'll explore different deployment tools and platforms, and guide you through the deployment process with one of the most popular platforms—**Heroku**.

1. Heroku

Heroku is a cloud platform that simplifies app deployment and scaling. It abstracts away much of the complexity of setting up infrastructure, making it an excellent choice for developers who want to focus on building their applications without managing servers. Heroku is widely used for its simplicity and ease of use, particularly for small to medium-sized projects.

Key Features of Heroku:

- Easy-to-use command-line interface (CLI) for deploying and managing apps.
- Supports multiple programming languages, including Python and Django.
- Built-in support for databases (e.g., PostgreSQL), file storage, and more.
- Automated scaling and monitoring.

2. DigitalOcean

DigitalOcean provides cloud infrastructure with a focus on simplicity and scalability. It offers virtual private servers (called "droplets") that you can configure and manage yourself. While it requires more manual configuration than Heroku, DigitalOcean provides more flexibility and control over the server environment.

Key Features of DigitalOcean:

- Affordable cloud hosting with flexible pricing.
- Full control over the server environment.
- Easy-to-use web dashboard and API for managing droplets.
- Supports various databases and technologies, including Django.

3. AWS (Amazon Web Services)

AWS is a comprehensive and powerful cloud platform with a wide range of services for compute, storage, databases, machine learning, and more. While it offers extensive features and scalability, it can be more complex to set up and manage than platforms like Heroku or DigitalOcean. AWS is ideal for large-scale applications that need to scale quickly and have high availability.

Key Features of AWS:

- Highly scalable and flexible infrastructure.
- A wide range of services, including EC2 (Elastic Compute Cloud) for hosting applications and RDS (Relational Database Service) for databases.
- Extensive tools for monitoring, security, and automation.

In this chapter, we'll focus on deploying a Django application to **Heroku** because of its ease of use and excellent support for Python applications.

Setting Up a Production Environment

Before deploying a Django application, you need to ensure that your **production environment** is properly set up. This involves configuring your settings, databases, static files, and ensuring that the application is secure.

1. Setting DEBUG to False

In development, Django's DEBUG mode is set to True, but in production, it must be set to False to prevent sensitive information from being exposed to users.

python

```
# settings.py
DEBUG = False
```

2. Setting ALLOWED_HOSTS

In production, you need to specify which hosts/domains your app can serve. This is done by setting the ALLOWED_HOSTS parameter in settings.py. It should be a list of hostnames that Django will allow to connect to the application.

python

```
# settings.py
ALLOWED_HOSTS = ['yourdomain.com',
'www.yourdomain.com']
```

3. Configuring Database Settings

For production, you'll likely use a database like **PostgreSQL** instead of SQLite (which is the default in Django's development environment). You'll need to install the `psycopg2` package and configure your database settings.

Install the PostgreSQL adapter:

bash

```
pip install psycopg2
```

Then, update your DATABASES setting in `settings.py`:

python

```
# settings.py

DATABASES = {
    'default': {
        'ENGINE':
'django.db.backends.postgresql',
        'NAME': 'yourdbname',
        'USER': 'yourdbuser',
        'PASSWORD': 'yourdbpassword',
        'HOST': 'yourdbhost',
        'PORT': '5432',
    }
```

}

4. Setting Up Static and Media Files

In production, static files (CSS, JavaScript, images) and media files (user-uploaded content) need to be served separately. Django's default file-serving mechanism is not suitable for production, so you'll need to configure it to use a web server like Nginx or a service like **Amazon S3** for serving these files.

For static files, you can use Django's `collectstatic` command to gather all static files into a single location:

```bash
bash
```

```bash
python manage.py collectstatic
```

In your production settings, you should configure the static and media file paths:

```python
python
```

```python
# settings.py

STATIC_URL = '/static/'
STATIC_ROOT = os.path.join(BASE_DIR, 'static')

MEDIA_URL = '/media/'
MEDIA_ROOT = os.path.join(BASE_DIR, 'media')
```

For production, it's common to use a service like Amazon S3 to store and serve media files.

5. Security Configuration

Make sure to set the following settings for added security:

- Use **HTTPS** (SSL/TLS) to encrypt traffic between the user and the server.
- Enable **CSRF protection** and **secure cookies**.
- Set SECURE_SSL_REDIRECT to True to force all HTTP traffic to be redirected to HTTPS.

python

```
# settings.py

SECURE_SSL_REDIRECT = True
SECURE_BROWSER_XSS_FILTER = True
SECURE_CONTENT_TYPE_NOSNIFF = True
```

Deploying a Django App with a Database

Now that the production environment is set up, we can proceed with deploying the Django app to a platform like **Heroku**. Here's a step-by-step guide to deploying a Django app on Heroku, including setting up a PostgreSQL database.

Step 1: Create a Heroku Account

First, sign up for a free Heroku account at Heroku's website. After that, install the Heroku CLI on your local machine.

Step 2: Install Heroku's Postgres Add-on

Heroku provides a managed PostgreSQL service. You can easily add it to your Django app with the following command:

bash

```
heroku addons:create heroku-postgresql:hobby-dev
```

This will provision a free PostgreSQL database for your app.

Step 3: Configure the Database for Heroku

Heroku automatically sets the DATABASE_URL environment variable to point to your PostgreSQL database. In your settings.py, modify the database settings to use this environment variable.

First, install the dj-database-url package:

bash

```
pip install dj-database-url
```

Then, update the DATABASES setting in settings.py:

```python
python

import dj_database_url

# settings.py

DATABASES = {
    'default':
dj_database_url.config(default='postgres://localhost')
}
```

This will allow Django to automatically use the DATABASE_URL environment variable for the database configuration.

Step 4: Prepare the Application for Deployment

Create a Procfile in the root of your project. This file tells Heroku how to run your application:

```makefile
makefile

web: gunicorn myproject.wsgi
```

Install **gunicorn** to serve your app:

```bash
bash
```

```
pip install gunicorn
```

Add the required dependencies to your `requirements.txt`:

```bash
pip freeze > requirements.txt
```

Also, make sure that you have `whitenoise` in your `requirements.txt` to handle static files in production:

```bash
pip install whitenoise
```

Then, add `whitenoise` to your `MIDDLEWARE` settings in `settings.py`:

```python
# settings.py

MIDDLEWARE = [

'whitenoise.middleware.WhiteNoiseMiddleware',  #
Add this line
    # other middleware
]
```

Step 5: Deploy to Heroku

1. **Login to Heroku**:

   ```bash
   heroku login
   ```

2. **Create a new Heroku app**:

   ```bash
   heroku create your-app-name
   ```

3. **Push your code to Heroku**:

   ```bash
   git push heroku master
   ```

4. **Run database migrations**:

   ```bash
   heroku run python manage.py migrate
   ```

5. **Collect static files**:

   ```bash
   ```

```
heroku run python manage.py collectstatic
```

Step 6: Access Your Django App

After deploying your Django app to Heroku, it will be available at a URL provided by Heroku (e.g., `https://your-app-name.herokuapp.com`). You can visit this URL in your browser to access your live app.

Real-World Example: Deploying a Blog App to Heroku

Let's apply all the steps to deploy a simple blog app to **Heroku**.

Step 1: Prepare Your Django App

- Make sure your Django app is ready for production, including configuring the database and static files, enabling HTTPS, and setting `DEBUG = False`.
- Create a `Procfile`, `requirements.txt`, and `runtime.txt` (if necessary).

Step 2: Deploy the App to Heroku

Follow the deployment steps outlined above to create the Heroku app, push your code, run the migrations, and collect static files.

Once your blog app is deployed, users can access it through the Heroku-provided URL. If you've set up database-backed blog posts and other features, they will work seamlessly.

Summary

In this chapter, we explored the process of deploying Django applications and configuring a production environment. We covered:

- Different **deployment tools** such as **Heroku**, **DigitalOcean**, and **AWS**, with a focus on **Heroku** for its simplicity.
- Setting up a **production environment**, including configuring settings for DEBUG, ALLOWED_HOSTS, databases, static files, and security.
- Deploying a Django app with a **PostgreSQL database** on Heroku.
- A **real-world example** of deploying a simple blog app to Heroku, including setting up a PostgreSQL database, static file handling, and deploying the app.

With the knowledge gained in this chapter, you can confidently deploy your Django applications to a production environment, ensuring they are secure, scalable, and ready for real-world use.

In the next chapter, we will explore **monitoring and maintaining Django applications** to ensure their continued reliability and performance in production.

CHAPTER 21

SCALING DJANGO WEB APPS FOR PERFORMANCE

Introduction to Scaling Django Applications

As your Django application grows and attracts more users, it becomes essential to ensure that your application can handle increased traffic and provide a smooth, responsive user experience. **Scaling** refers to the process of improving the performance and capacity of your application to handle a larger load. There are two main types of scaling:

- **Vertical scaling** (scaling up): Adding more resources (e.g., CPU, RAM) to a single server.
- **Horizontal scaling** (scaling out): Distributing the load across multiple servers.

For Django applications, scaling involves optimizing the infrastructure, web servers, databases, and caching strategies to ensure your app can handle traffic spikes and remain performant under heavy load.

In this chapter, we'll focus on the key strategies to scale a Django web application:

1. **Load balancing**: Distributing traffic across multiple servers.

2. **Caching**: Reducing load on your web servers and databases by storing frequently accessed data.

3. **Database optimization**: Ensuring your database can handle high traffic and queries efficiently.

By implementing these strategies, you can significantly improve your Django app's ability to handle large amounts of traffic and provide a better user experience.

Load Balancing, Caching, and Database Optimization

1. Load Balancing

Load balancing is the process of distributing incoming traffic across multiple servers to ensure no single server is overwhelmed. When traffic spikes occur, a load balancer automatically distributes the requests to the available servers, ensuring that each server is utilized efficiently.

How to implement load balancing in Django:

- **Reverse Proxy**: One common approach is to use a reverse proxy server like **Nginx** or **HAProxy** to handle incoming requests and distribute them across multiple Django application servers.

- **Horizontal Scaling**: You can scale your Django application horizontally by deploying multiple instances of your Django app on different servers or containers. The reverse proxy server then balances the load between these instances.
- **Auto-scaling**: In cloud environments (e.g., AWS, Google Cloud), you can set up auto-scaling, which automatically adjusts the number of running instances based on traffic patterns.

Example of a reverse proxy setup using **Nginx**:

```nginx
http {
    upstream django_app {
        server  192.168.1.2:8000;      #  Django
instance 1
        server  192.168.1.3:8000;      #  Django
instance 2
    }

    server {
        location / {
            proxy_pass http://django_app;
            proxy_set_header Host $host;
            proxy_set_header           X-Real-IP
$remote_addr;
```

```
        proxy_set_header        X-Forwarded-For
$proxy_add_x_forwarded_for;
        proxy_set_header     X-Forwarded-Proto
$scheme;
        }
    }
}
```

In this configuration, Nginx is acting as a load balancer, distributing traffic between two Django application instances.

2. Caching

Caching is one of the most effective ways to improve the performance of your Django application. Caching reduces the need to repeatedly fetch data from the database, which can be time-consuming and resource-intensive.

Django provides several caching strategies:

- **Page caching**: Caching the entire response of a view.
- **Template caching**: Caching the rendered output of a template.
- **Database query caching**: Storing results from database queries in memory to avoid redundant database calls.
- **Fragment caching**: Caching a portion of a page (useful for sections of a page that don't change often).

How to implement caching in Django:

247

1. **Page Caching**: Use the `cache_page` decorator to cache entire views.

```python
python

from django.views.decorators.cache import cache_page
from django.shortcuts import render

@cache_page(60 * 15)    # Cache for 15 minutes
def blog_list_view(request):
    posts = BlogPost.objects.all()
    return                  render(request,
'blog/blog_list.html', {'posts': posts})
```

2. **Template Fragment Caching**: Cache parts of a page, such as a list of blog posts that rarely change.

```html
html

{% load cache %}
{% cache 600 blog_posts %}
    <ul>
    {% for post in posts %}
        <li>{{ post.title }}</li>
    {% endfor %}
    </ul>
{% endcache %}
```

3. **Database Query Caching**: Cache the results of expensive queries using Django's caching framework.

```python
from django.core.cache import cache
def get_popular_posts():
    popular_posts                              =
cache.get('popular_posts')
    if not popular_posts:
        popular_posts                          =
BlogPost.objects.filter(popular=True)
        cache.set('popular_posts',
popular_posts, timeout=60*15)  # Cache for
15 minutes
    return popular_posts
```

Choosing the Right Caching Strategy:

- Use **page caching** for views that don't change frequently, such as static pages.
- Use **template fragment caching** for sections of a page that can be cached separately.
- Use **database query caching** to cache expensive database queries and reduce load on the database.

3. Database Optimization

As your application scales, optimizing the database becomes crucial to ensure that it can handle large volumes of data and queries efficiently. Here are some key strategies for optimizing your Django database:

1. **Indexing**: Use database indexes on frequently queried fields to speed up query execution. For example, if you frequently filter blog posts by `author`, consider adding an index to the `author` field.

    python

    ```python
    class BlogPost(models.Model):
        title                    =
    models.CharField(max_length=200)
        author                   =
    models.CharField(max_length=100,
    db_index=True)  # Index added
    ```

2. **Query Optimization**: Avoid **N+1 queries**, where a separate database query is made for each related object. Use **select_related** (for single-valued relationships) and **prefetch_related** (for multi-valued relationships) to fetch related objects in a single query.

    python

```
# Avoid N+1 queries
posts                                    =
BlogPost.objects.select_related('author')
.all()
```

3. **Database Sharding**: As your database grows, you may need to distribute data across multiple databases or partitions. This is known as **sharding** and can help scale your database to handle massive amounts of data.

4. **Database Connection Pooling**: Use connection pooling to manage database connections efficiently. This reduces the overhead of opening and closing database connections on every request.

Real-World Example: Scaling a Blog App to Handle Traffic Spikes

Let's apply these scaling strategies to a **blog app** that needs to handle traffic spikes. We'll implement the following strategies:

1. **Load balancing** with multiple application servers.
2. **Caching** to speed up view rendering and reduce database load.
3. **Database optimization** to handle high volumes of data and queries.

Step 1: Implement Load Balancing

We set up multiple Django application instances on different servers and use **Nginx** as a reverse proxy to distribute the traffic between them. The Nginx configuration ensures that traffic is distributed evenly, and if one server fails, the other can handle the requests.

Step 2: Implement Caching

We use **page caching** for the blog list view to avoid querying the database on every request. This is particularly useful for handling traffic spikes when many users request the same page:

python

```python
from django.views.decorators.cache import cache_page

@cache_page(60 * 15)  # Cache for 15 minutes
def blog_list_view(request):
    posts = BlogPost.objects.all()
    return render(request, 'blog/blog_list.html', {'posts': posts})
```

For frequently accessed content, such as the most popular blog posts, we use **database query caching**:

python

```python
from django.core.cache import cache

def get_popular_posts():
    popular_posts = cache.get('popular_posts')
    if not popular_posts:
        popular_posts                          =
BlogPost.objects.filter(popular=True)
        cache.set('popular_posts',
popular_posts, timeout=60*15)   # Cache for 15
minutes
    return popular_posts
```

Step 3: Optimize Database Queries

We use **select_related** to optimize queries that involve related models. For example, if we need to list blog posts along with their authors, we can use `select_related` to minimize database queries:

```
python
```

```python
def blog_list_view(request):
    posts                                       =
BlogPost.objects.select_related('author').all()
    return                          render(request,
'blog/blog_list.html', {'posts': posts})
```

Additionally, we add indexes to fields that are frequently used for filtering, such as `author`:

```python
python

class BlogPost(models.Model):
    title = models.CharField(max_length=200)
    author = models.CharField(max_length=100,
db_index=True)  # Index added
```

Step 4: Prepare for Traffic Spikes

When deploying the blog app, we configure **auto-scaling** on the server (e.g., Heroku, AWS EC2) to automatically spin up additional instances of the application during traffic spikes. This ensures that the application can handle increased load without manual intervention.

Summary

In this chapter, we explored strategies for **scaling Django applications** to handle increased traffic and performance demands:

- **Load balancing** distributes traffic across multiple servers, ensuring your app can handle high volumes of requests.
- **Caching** reduces database load and speeds up page rendering, making your app more responsive under high traffic.

- **Database optimization** ensures your database can efficiently handle large datasets and complex queries.

We applied these strategies to a **real-world example** by scaling a blog app, setting up load balancing, implementing caching, and optimizing database queries. By using these techniques, you can ensure your Django application remains performant and scalable as traffic increases.

In the next chapter, we will discuss **monitoring and logging** to keep track of your Django application's performance and health in production.

CHAPTER 22

ASYNCHRONOUS PROCESSING IN DJANGO

Introduction to Asynchronous Tasks in Django

In modern web applications, certain tasks—such as sending emails, processing images, or performing time-consuming calculations—can significantly slow down the user experience if performed synchronously. These tasks can cause delays in page loading times, which leads to a poor user experience.

Asynchronous processing allows you to offload these long-running tasks to be processed in the background, freeing up resources for handling other user requests. By performing tasks asynchronously, you can keep the web application responsive and provide a better overall experience.

Django, by default, is synchronous. However, Django supports asynchronous processing through various tools and techniques, with **Celery** being one of the most popular libraries for handling background tasks in Django.

In this chapter, we will:

1. Introduce **asynchronous tasks** in Django and the concept of background task processing.
2. Show how to use **Celery** for asynchronous task processing.
3. Provide a real-world example of implementing asynchronous email notifications in Django.

Using Celery for Background Task Processing

Celery is an open-source asynchronous task queue/job queue system that is widely used for managing background tasks in Django applications. Celery uses message brokers (such as **RabbitMQ** or **Redis**) to handle task queues and distribute the work to worker processes.

Step 1: Installing Celery and a Message Broker

To get started with Celery, you need to install Celery and a message broker. For this example, we'll use **Redis** as the message broker.

First, install **Celery** and **Redis**:

bash

```
pip install celery redis
```

Then, install **Redis** on your system. You can install Redis via a package manager like `apt` on Ubuntu or `brew` on macOS.

Step 2: Configuring Celery in Your Django Project

In your Django project directory, create a new file called `celery.py`. This file will contain the Celery configuration and initialization code.

```python
# myproject/celery.py

import os
from celery import Celery

# Set the default Django settings module for the
'celery' program.
os.environ.setdefault('DJANGO_SETTINGS_MODULE',
'myproject.settings')

app = Celery('myproject')

# Using a string here means the worker doesn't
have to serialize
# the configuration object to child processes.
# - namespace='CELERY' means all celery-related
config keys should have a `CELERY_` prefix.
```

```
app.config_from_object('django.conf:settings',
namespace='CELERY')

# Load task modules from all registered Django
app configs.
app.autodiscover_tasks()
```

In this file:

- **Celery('myproject')** initializes the Celery instance with the name of your Django project.
- **app.config_from_object('django.conf:settings', namespace='CELERY')** loads the Celery configuration from your Django settings, specifically settings with the prefix CELERY_.
- **app.autodiscover_tasks()** allows Celery to discover tasks in your Django apps automatically.

Next, update your **__init__.py** file in the main project directory (myproject/__init__.py) to ensure that Celery is loaded when Django starts:

```python

# myproject/__init__.py

from __future__ import absolute_import,
unicode_literals
```

```
# This will make sure the app is always imported
when
# Django starts so that shared_task will use this
app.
from .celery import app as celery_app

__all__ = ('celery_app',)
```

Step 3: Configuring Celery in Django Settings

In settings.py, you need to configure the message broker (e.g., Redis) for Celery:

```python
# settings.py

# Celery configuration
CELERY_BROKER_URL = 'redis://localhost:6379/0'
# Redis broker URL
CELERY_ACCEPT_CONTENT = ['json']
CELERY_TASK_SERIALIZER = 'json'
CELERY_RESULT_BACKEND                        =
'redis://localhost:6379/0'  # Redis backend for
storing results
```

In this example:

- **CELERY_BROKER_URL** points to the Redis instance, which will act as the broker for the Celery tasks.

- **CELERY_RESULT_BACKEND** tells Celery where to store the results of tasks. In this case, we are using Redis as both the broker and the result backend.

Step 4: Creating Celery Tasks

Now you can create tasks that will run asynchronously. Celery tasks are simple Python functions that you decorate with the @app.task decorator.

For example, let's create a task to send an email asynchronously.

In your Django app (blog in this case), create a file called tasks.py:

python

```
# blog/tasks.py

from celery import shared_task
from django.core.mail import send_mail

@shared_task
def send_welcome_email(user_email):
    send_mail(
        'Welcome to our Blog!',
        'Thank you for signing up.',
        'from@example.com',
        [user_email],
```

261

```
        fail_silently=False,
    )
```

In this example:

- The `send_welcome_email` function is a Celery task that sends a welcome email asynchronously.
- We use Django's `send_mail` function to send the email.
- The `@shared_task` decorator marks this function as a Celery task that can be executed in the background.

Step 5: Running the Celery Worker

To process the tasks in the background, you need to run the **Celery worker** process. In your project directory, run the following command:

```bash
bash
```

```
celery -A myproject worker --loglevel=info
```

This starts the Celery worker, which will listen for tasks in the queue and process them as they come in.

Step 6: Calling the Celery Task

Now that we have the task set up, you can call it from any view or function in your Django app. For example, to send a welcome email after a user registers:

```python
python

# views.py

from django.shortcuts import render
from django.http import HttpResponse
from .tasks import send_welcome_email

def register(request):
    if request.method == 'POST':
        # Assuming user is registered successfully
        user_email = request.POST.get('email')
        # Call the Celery task to send the welcome email asynchronously
        send_welcome_email.delay(user_email)
        return HttpResponse("Registration successful! A welcome email will be sent shortly.")
    return render(request, 'register.html')
```

In this example:

- When a user registers, we use `send_welcome_email.delay(user_email)` to send the email asynchronously. The `delay()` method is used to send the task to the Celery worker.

Step 7: Viewing Task Results

If you want to check the result of a task (e.g., to see if it was successful), you can use the **AsyncResult** object:

```python
from celery.result import AsyncResult

# Get the result of a task by its ID
result = AsyncResult(task_id)
if result.successful():
    print("Task completed successfully.")
```

Real-World Example: Sending Email Notifications Asynchronously

In a real-world Django application, sending email notifications (such as a welcome email after registration) can be time-consuming, especially if the email service is slow or there are many users. By sending emails asynchronously using Celery, we can improve the performance of the application and ensure the registration process remains fast and responsive.

Step 1: Set Up Celery with Django

- Install Celery and configure it with Redis as the message broker.

- Update `settings.py` to configure the Celery broker and result backend.

Step 2: Create Celery Tasks

- Create a task to send emails asynchronously using the `send_mail` function in Django.

Step 3: Call the Celery Task

- Call the task from your view using the `.delay()` method to execute it in the background.

Step 4: Running the Celery Worker

- Run the Celery worker to process background tasks.

Summary

In this chapter, we explored **asynchronous processing** in Django and how to use **Celery** to handle background tasks. We covered:

- **Asynchronous tasks** in Django: Offloading time-consuming tasks to run in the background to improve the responsiveness of your application.
- **Celery**: A powerful tool for handling asynchronous tasks, with Redis as the message broker.

265

- **Real-world example**: Implementing Celery to send email notifications asynchronously for a blog app.

By using Celery for background task processing, you can ensure that your Django application remains responsive, even when handling long-running tasks. In the next chapter, we will explore **WebSockets and real-time communication** in Django to handle scenarios like live updates and chat applications.

CHAPTER 23

USING THIRD-PARTY LIBRARIES AND DJANGO PACKAGES

Introduction to Useful Django Packages and Libraries

Django is a robust web framework that provides many built-in features for developing web applications, but its ecosystem also includes a wide range of third-party packages and libraries that can significantly extend its functionality. These packages can help you solve common problems, improve productivity, and add powerful features to your Django application with minimal effort.

Some common use cases for third-party Django libraries include:

- **Authentication**: Implementing custom user authentication methods (e.g., OAuth, social login).
- **Search functionality**: Adding advanced search capabilities to your application.
- **Form handling**: Enhancing Django's built-in form handling with features like drag-and-drop file uploads, or multi-step forms.
- **API development**: Building robust APIs with frameworks like Django Rest Framework (DRF).

- **Testing**: Writing more effective and comprehensive tests with testing libraries.

- **Admin customization**: Extending the default Django admin interface with additional features and customizations.

In this chapter, we'll explore how to integrate third-party libraries into a Django project. We'll focus on adding **search functionality** to a blog app using **Elasticsearch**, a powerful and scalable search engine.

Installing and Using Third-Party Packages

Step 1: Finding and Installing Django Packages

To find the right package for your needs, you can visit the Django Packages website (https://djangopackages.org/) or browse GitHub for popular open-source Django projects. Once you've found the right package, installing it is straightforward using **pip**, the Python package manager.

For example, to install a third-party Django package like **django-elasticsearch-dsl** (a package that integrates Elasticsearch with Django), you can run the following command:

```bash
pip install django-elasticsearch-dsl
```

This will install the package and any dependencies required. After installation, you can add the package to your INSTALLED_APPS in settings.py if necessary:

```python

# settings.py

INSTALLED_APPS = [
    # other apps
    'django_elasticsearch_dsl',
]
```

Django packages often come with additional setup instructions, such as configuration settings or commands to run. Be sure to check the documentation of each package for any specific installation or configuration requirements.

Step 2: Adding a Package to Your Project

Once the package is installed, you can begin using it in your Django project. For example, when using **django-elasticsearch-dsl**, you would need to configure the connection to Elasticsearch and define search-related models.

Real-World Example: Adding a Search Function to Your Blog with Elasticsearch

In this example, we'll add **Elasticsearch** search functionality to a blog app. Elasticsearch is a distributed search engine that provides full-text search capabilities, which are faster and more flexible than traditional SQL queries for search use cases.

Step 1: Install Elasticsearch and Django Elasticsearch DSL

To integrate Elasticsearch with Django, we'll use the `django-elasticsearch-dsl` package. This package provides an easy-to-use wrapper around the official Elasticsearch Python client, allowing you to define search indexes as Django models.

First, install **Elasticsearch** on your machine:

```bash

# On Ubuntu
sudo apt-get install elasticsearch
```

Next, install the **django-elasticsearch-dsl** package:

```bash

pip install django-elasticsearch-dsl
```

Step 2: Configure Elasticsearch in settings.py

In settings.py, configure the connection to your Elasticsearch instance:

python

```
# settings.py

ELASTICSEARCH_DSL = {
    'default': {
        'HOST': 'localhost:9200',    # Default
Elasticsearch host
    },
}
```

This will connect Django to a locally running Elasticsearch server. You can customize the host and port as needed if you're using a hosted Elasticsearch service.

Step 3: Create an Elasticsearch Document for the BlogPost Model

Next, create an Elasticsearch **Document** for your BlogPost model. In documents.py (inside your app directory), define the BlogPostDocument class:

python

```
# documents.py
```

```
from django_elasticsearch_dsl import Document,
fields
from django_elasticsearch_dsl.registries import
registry
from .models import BlogPost


@registry.register_document
class BlogPostDocument(Document):
    title = fields.TextField()
    content = fields.TextField()

    class Index:
        # Name of the Elasticsearch index
        name = 'blogposts'

    class Django:
        model = BlogPost  # The model that the
document is based on
        fields = ['title', 'content']  # The
fields to be indexed
```

In this document:

- title and content fields are indexed to enable full-text search.
- The name attribute defines the name of the Elasticsearch index.

- The `model` attribute specifies the Django model the document is associated with.

Step 4: Create the Search View

Now that Elasticsearch is configured, create a view that handles search queries. In `views.py`, create a view to allow users to search for blog posts:

python

```python
# views.py

from django.shortcuts import render
from django.http import HttpResponse
from .documents import BlogPostDocument

def search_view(request):
    query = request.GET.get('q', '')   # Get the
search query from the URL parameters
    results                              =
BlogPostDocument.search().query('match',
content=query) if query else []
    return                      render(request,
'blog/search_results.html', {'results': results,
'query': query})
```

In this view:

- We retrieve the search query from the URL using `request.GET.get('q', '')`.
- We perform a `match` query on the `content` field of the `BlogPostDocument` to find posts that match the search query.
- We pass the search results to the template.

Step 5: Create the Search Template

Now, create a template to display the search results. In `search_results.html`, display the search query and the results:

html

```
<!-- search_results.html -->

<h1>Search Results for "{{ query }}"</h1>

{% if results %}
    <ul>
        {% for post in results %}
            <li><a href="{% url 'blog_detail'
post.id %}">{{ post.title }}</a></li>
        {% endfor %}
    </ul>
{% else %}
    <p>No results found.</p>
{% endif %}
```

In this template:

- We display the search query and list the titles of blog posts that match the search query.
- Each result links to the corresponding blog post's detail page.

Step 6: Configure URL Patterns

In `urls.py`, create a URL pattern for the search view:

python

```
# urls.py

from django.urls import path
from . import views

urlpatterns = [
    # other URLs
    path('search/',            views.search_view,
name='search'),
]
```

Now, you can search for blog posts by visiting `/search/?q=your-query`.

Step 7: Indexing Data in Elasticsearch

Before you can search your blog posts in Elasticsearch, you need to **index** the existing data. To do this, run the following management command:

```bash

python manage.py search_index --create   # Create the Elasticsearch index
python manage.py search_index --populate   # Populate the index with existing data
```

This will index the data in your database and make it available for search.

Testing and Scaling the Search Feature

Once the search function is up and running, you should test it to ensure it works as expected:

- Perform a few test searches and verify that the search results match the query.
- Ensure that the search function is fast and responsive, even as the number of blog posts grows.

For scaling:

- As the volume of data in Elasticsearch grows, consider optimizing the queries and ensuring your Elasticsearch cluster is configured for high availability.
- You may need to periodically reindex data if there are significant changes to the data structure or content.

Summary

In this chapter, we explored how to use **third-party libraries and Django packages** to extend the functionality of your application. We focused on integrating **Elasticsearch** with Django to add advanced search functionality to a blog app. Key topics covered include:

- **Installing and configuring third-party packages** like `django-elasticsearch-dsl` to integrate Elasticsearch with Django.
- **Creating Elasticsearch documents** to index model data and perform full-text searches.
- **Implementing a search view and template** to allow users to search blog posts by content.
- **Indexing data** and testing the search functionality.

By integrating Elasticsearch, you can significantly improve the search experience in your Django application, making it more powerful and responsive. In the next chapter, we'll explore **continuous integration (CI) and continuous deployment (CD)** to automate testing and deployment workflows for your Django projects.

CHAPTER 24

INTERNATIONALIZATION (I18N) AND LOCALIZATION (L10N)

Introduction to Internationalization (i18n) and Localization (l10n)

In today's globalized world, web applications need to be accessible to users from different countries, cultures, and languages. **Internationalization (i18n)** and **localization (l10n)** are two key concepts that help achieve this goal.

- **Internationalization (i18n)** refers to the process of designing and developing a web application so that it can be easily adapted to different languages, regions, and cultures without requiring changes to the core code.
- **Localization (l10n)** refers to the actual adaptation of the application for a specific locale, such as translating text, formatting dates and numbers, and adjusting the layout for right-to-left (RTL) languages.

Django provides robust support for both i18n and l10n, allowing developers to build web applications that are easily translatable and can serve users in different regions and languages.

In this chapter, we'll cover:

1. **Internationalizing and localizing Django applications** using Django's built-in tools.

2. **Translating content** and handling time zones to ensure that the application is accessible to a global audience.

3. A **real-world example** of building a **multi-language blog app** that serves content in different languages.

Internationalizing and Localizing Django Applications

1. Internationalizing Your Django Application

To internationalize your Django application, you need to ensure that your application can support multiple languages. Django provides tools to mark strings for translation and prepare your application for localization.

Step 1: Enable Locale Middleware

First, enable the **LocaleMiddleware** in your MIDDLEWARE setting in settings.py to manage language preferences based on user sessions or browser settings.

```python

# settings.py

MIDDLEWARE = [
    # other middleware
```

```
'django.middleware.locale.LocaleMiddleware',    #
Add this middleware for language selection
]
```

Step 2: Set up Available Languages

Django allows you to define the languages your application supports. Add the LANGUAGES setting in settings.py to specify the available languages:

```python
# settings.py

LANGUAGES = [
    ('en', 'English'),
    ('es', 'Spanish'),
    ('fr', 'French'),
    ('de', 'German'),
    ('pt', 'Portuguese'),
]

# Default language
LANGUAGE_CODE = 'en'
```

This configuration supports English, Spanish, French, German, and Portuguese in your application, with English set as the default language.

Step 3: Mark Strings for Translation

In Django, you can mark strings for translation using the `gettext` function (`_()` is the alias for `gettext`). These strings will be translated into the user's preferred language.

To use translation functions, import `gettext` or `ugettext`:

```python
# views.py
from django.utils.translation import gettext as
_

def my_view(request):
    greeting = _("Welcome to the blog!")
    return      render(request,      'home.html',
{'greeting': greeting})
```

In this example, the string `"Welcome to the blog!"` is marked for translation.

2. Localization in Django

Localization refers to the actual transformation of the application to meet the needs of specific locales, such as translating text and adjusting formatting for dates, numbers, and currencies.

Step 1: Time Zones and Localized Dates

Django makes it easy to manage time zones and localized date formatting. To enable time zone support, set USE_TZ to True and configure the time zone in settings.py:

python

```
# settings.py

USE_TZ = True  # Enable time zone support
TIME_ZONE = 'UTC'  # Default time zone
```

To allow users to use their local time zone, you can enable **time zone switching** using the timezone module:

python

```
from django.utils import timezone

def my_view(request):
    local_time                                =
timezone.localtime(timezone.now())    # Get the
local time
    return        render(request,        'home.html',
{'local_time': local_time})
```

Step 2: Localizing Numbers and Currencies

Django also supports localizing numbers and currencies. Use the `localize` function to format numbers and currencies based on the user's locale.

```python

from django.utils import formats

# Format a number as currency
amount = 12345.67
localized_amount = formats.localize(amount)
```

The format of the number will be adjusted based on the selected locale (e.g., using commas or periods as thousand separators, adjusting currency symbols, etc.).

Translating Content and Handling Time Zones

1. Translating Content

Django provides a built-in **translation** framework to translate static content and model fields. To create translation files, use Django's **makemessages** command to extract translatable strings.

Step 1: Generate Translation Files

Run the following command to generate `.po` files, which contain the translatable strings:

```bash
```

```bash
django-admin makemessages -l es    # Create
translation files for Spanish
```

This will generate a `.po` file under the `locale` directory for the specified language (`es` for Spanish).

Step 2: Edit the `.po` File

Open the generated `.po` file in the `locale/es/LC_MESSAGES` directory and add the translations for each string:

```po
```

```po
msgid "Welcome to the blog!"
msgstr "¡Bienvenido al blog!"
```

Step 3: Compile Translation Files

Once you've added the translations, compile them into `.mo` files that Django can use:

```bash
```

```bash
django-admin compilemessages
```

Step 4: Switch Languages in Views

To switch languages dynamically in Django, you can use `set_language` in your views to change the language based on user input or preferences:

```python
from django.shortcuts import render
from django.utils.translation import activate

def set_language_view(request, lang_code):
    activate(lang_code)  # Activate the language
code (e.g., 'es' for Spanish)
    return render(request, 'home.html')
```

Real-World Example: Building a Multi-Language Blog App

Let's build a **multi-language blog app** that supports multiple languages and dynamically switches between them. The app will allow users to view blog posts in different languages and will display the blog content in the selected language.

Step 1: Set Up the Blog Model

First, we need to create a `BlogPost` model where each post will have a title and content in multiple languages.

```python
# models.py

from django.db import models
from django.utils.translation import gettext_lazy as _

class BlogPost(models.Model):
    title = models.CharField(max_length=200)
    content = models.TextField()
    created_at = models.DateTimeField(auto_now_add=True)

    def __str__(self):
        return self.title
```

Step 2: Create a View to Display Blog Posts

Next, create a view that will render the blog posts in the user's selected language.

```python
# views.py

from django.shortcuts import render
from .models import BlogPost
from django.utils.translation import activate
```

```python
def blog_list_view(request):
    # Get the user's selected language from the
session or default to English
    lang_code = request.GET.get('lang', 'en')
    activate(lang_code)

    # Fetch all blog posts
    posts = BlogPost.objects.all()
    return                        render(request,
'blog/blog_list.html', {'posts': posts})
```

Step 3: Add Translation to Blog Templates

In the template, we will render the blog posts, and dynamically display them in the selected language.

html

```html
<!-- blog_list.html -->

<h1>{% trans "Blog Posts" %}</h1>

<ul>
    {% for post in posts %}
        <li>
            <h2>{{ post.title }}</h2>
            <p>{{ post.content }}</p>
        </li>
    {% endfor %}
</ul>
```

```
<form method="get">
    <select name="lang">
        <option value="en">English</option>
        <option value="es">Español</option>
        <option value="fr">Français</option>
    </select>
    <button type="submit">{% trans "Change
Language" %}</button>
</form>
```

In this template:

- We use {% trans "Blog Posts" %} to translate the static text.
- The form allows users to switch between English, Spanish, and French.

Step 4: Generate and Compile Translations

Run the makemessages and compilemessages commands to generate translation files for your chosen languages (English, Spanish, and French).

bash

```
django-admin makemessages -l es   # Spanish
django-admin makemessages -l fr   # French
django-admin compilemessages
```

After editing the .po files with the appropriate translations, you can compile them into .mo files and restart the server to view the content in different languages.

Summary

In this chapter, we explored the concepts of **Internationalization (i18n)** and **Localization (l10n)** in Django, and how to build a Django application that supports multiple languages and regions. We covered:

- **Internationalizing a Django application** by marking strings for translation and configuring language settings.
- **Localizing content** by formatting dates, numbers, and currencies to fit the locale.
- A **real-world example** of building a **multi-language blog app**, where users can select their preferred language to view blog posts.
- **Generating and compiling translation files** using Django's `makemessages` and `compilemessages` commands.

By implementing these features, your Django application can easily serve a global audience, providing a localized and personalized user experience. In the next chapter, we will cover

Testing in Django, ensuring that your application is robust, reliable, and ready for production.

www.ingramcontent.com/pod-product-compliance
Lightning Source LLC
LaVergne TN
LVHW051436050326
832903LV00030BD/3108